# Habitat, Health, and Development

# Habitat, Health, and Development

## A NEW WAY OF LOOKING AT CITIES IN THE THIRD WORLD

EDITED BY
## JOSEPH S. TULCHIN

Lynne Rienner Publishers, Inc.
Boulder, Colorado

Published in the United States of America by
Lynne Rienner Publishers, Inc.
948 North Street, Boulder, Colorado 80302

**Library of Congress Cataloging-in-Publication Data**
Main entry under title:

Habitat, health, and development.

   1. Urban health—Developing countries.   2. Squatter
settlements—Developing countries.   3. Housing and
health—Developing countries.   I. Tulchin, Joseph S.,
1939-   .
RA566.5.D44H33   1985        362.1'09172'4        85-19604
ISBN 0-931477-50-6

Distributed outside of North and South America and Japan by
Frances Pinter (Publishers) Ltd, 25 Floral Street,
London WC2E 9DS England.  UK ISBN 0-86187-592-3

Printed and bound in the United States of America

# Contents

# Figures and Tables

# Preface

This book is the fruit of a casual conversation I had
with Jorge Enrique Hardoy nearly five years ago.
Hardoy, who has spent the past twenty-five years studying urban problems in the Third World, was describing to
me the work his multinational network was doing on small
towns and intermediate cities, under the auspices of the
International Institute for Environment and Development
(IIED, London). He had set up teams in India, the
Sudan, Nigeria, and Argentina with the same research in-
tentions and questions, and he discovered, though not to
his surprise, that the patterns of human settlement were
remarkably similar throughout the Third World and that
the shantytowns that had come to dominate the urban
landscape in Latin America, Africa, the Middle East, and
Asia played a critical role in contemporary urban
experience.

Hardoy had found the collaborative experience im-
mensely rewarding and had hopes that it might have an
impact on the policies of national and international
agencies concerned with settlement issues. Several international funding agencies, both private and public,
had come to understand the significance of the popular
settlements and were willing to fund urban research that
focused on those nonlegal and illegal communities, especially their strategies for survival and their
residents' linkages to the labor market and other segments of the formal or legal society.

In all the work done by these various teams, Hardoy was struck by the centrality of health and the
preoccupation of popular settlement inhabitants with
health. He and his colleagues were sensitive enough to
observe the consequences of poverty for the health of
settlement inhabitants, but none of them was trained
specifically to evaluate the health dimension of settlement decisions or settlement organization. Hardoy

believed that, in order for research on popular settlements to be useful and to have the impact he desired on the policy process, it was necessary to evaluate systematically the health consequences of settlement patterns.

A major research university seemed the ideal context for such a multidisciplinary approach, and so to begin an inquiry into the health aspects of human settlement patterns, I contacted James W. Lea, director of the Office of International Affairs of the School of Medicine at the University of North Carolina at Chapel Hill, and Jonathan B. Howes, director of the Center for Urban and Regional Studies at UNC-CH. Together, we organized a series of informal luncheons for faculty across our campus who seemed to have some expertise on one facet or another of this complex subject. We organized the gatherings to coincide with the travel plans of Hardoy, on his rounds of the international organizations with which he is affiliated. Two conclusions emerged from this series of conversations. First, that planners or specialist in settlement issues and health specialists rarely talked to one another professionally in a systematic fashion, so that the topic as we had defined it was essentially unexplored. Second, that both groups agreed enthusiastically that their work would be enhanced by better communication between them and that, in the Third World, urban issues and health issues were inextricably intertwined. Indeed, some of us had come to suspect that research on urban problems would require systematic consideration of health variables. The issue, as we came to understand it, was how health questions should be integrated with settlement or habitat questions in a useful and viable research design.

To solve this last dilemma, we decided to hold a conference in Chapel Hill in June 1983 in which health and habitat specialists would meet to summarize what we already knew about the overlap between the two fields. The objective of the conference was to frame a research design that would serve as the basis for future funding proposals by scholars in the United States and by the international network of teams working under Hardoy's leadership in the IIED. We commissioned papers on different facets of the problem and a set of case studies on work being done in various parts of the world, and invited as discussants specialists who had had field experience that put them in a position to comment on the multidisciplinary project we were trying to formulate. The papers were not intended as formal, scholarly treatises. They were designed as stimuli for discussion among specialists from different disciplines, and we expected that we might learn as much from the informal exchanges that followed each set of papers as from the papers themselves. The tone of the conference was kept informal in order to encourage exchange. Because of the original intention, and because we believe that the discussions contain some of the most innovative insights, we have included them in this volume.

The papers in this volume, with one exception, have been edited from the transcript of the conference. That exception is the chapter by John Briscoe, who had to withdraw from the conference at the very last minute and who had prepared a paper on water and health, which he was kind enough to permit us to include. Other presentations by health specialists were by Donald Madison, Daniel A. Okun, Cecil G. Sheps, C. Arden Miller, and Guy Steuart of the Schools of Medicine and Public Health at UNC-CH. General presentations by planners were given by Hardoy and David Satterthwaite of the London office of IIED. Three case studies were included, two by members of the IIED network, Cesar Vapnarsky and H. N. Misra, and one by Luis Sierra, a member of the United Nations Center for Human Settlements and Habitat. In addition, health specialists and planners were invited to participate as discussants. Their names are given in the list of participants.

The papers of the conference and the discussion, here transformed into a book, represent a conscious collective effort at paradigm shock. In the months since our meeting, we have continued to mull over the implications of our exchanges. Our objective was, and remains, to define a new program of research that will combine the insights of the health field with the insights of those concerned with habitat. We have made some progress. Together with members of the UNC-CH faculty we have drafted a research proposal with the title "Health and Habitat" that we hope will catch the attention of the appropriate funding agency. Even as we continue to polish and refine our efforts, the World Health Organization has recognized the importance of habitat for its work, and the housing agencies of several governments have acknowledged the significance of health issues for their policy efforts. Thus, although we cannot claim to have accomplished our goals, we have begun. We hope this book serves the purpose of stimulating thought among scholars in many different disciplines, policymakers concerned with the well-being of the world's poor, and all those with an interest in the Third World.

Joseph S. Tulchin
Chapel Hill

# Participants

**William Alonso** is Director of the Center for population Studies, Harvard University.

**Carole Crumley** is Associate Professor of Anthropology, University of North Carolina at Chapel Hill.

**Benjamin Fisher** is Staff Consultant for the World Bank, Washington, D.C.

**Jorge Enrique Hardoy** is Senior Researcher at the Centro de Estudios Urbanos y Regionales, Buenos Aires, Argentina, and Director of the Human Settlements Project of the International Institute of Environment and Development.

**Jonathan B. Howes** is Director of the Center of Urban and Regional Studies, University of North Carolina at Chapel Hill.

**Jaroslav Hulka** is Professor of Obstetrics and Gynecology, the School of Medicine, University of North Carolina at Chapel Hill.

**Linda Lacey** is Associate Professor of City and Regional Planning, University of North Carolina at Chapel Hill.

**Donald L. Madison** is Professor of Social and Administrative Medicine, School of Medicine, University of North Carolina at Chapel Hill.

**C. Arden Miller** is Professor and Chairman of the Department of Maternal and Child Health School of Public Health, University of North Carolina at Chapel Hill.

**H. N. Misra** is Director of the International Institute for Development Research, Allahabad, India.

**Caroline O. N. Moser** is a member of the Development Planning Unit, University College, London, England.

**Daniel A. Okun** is Kenan Professor Emeritus of Environmental Science and Engineering, School of Public Health, University of North Carolina at Chapel Hill.

**William Rohe** is Assistant Professor of City and Regional Planning, University of North Carolina at Chapel Hill.

**David Satterthwaite** is Senior Staff Associate of the International Institute of Environment and Development, London, England.

**Luis Sierra** is a staff member of the United Nations Center for Human Settlements and Habitat.

**Guy W. Steuart** is Professor and Chairman of the Department of Health Education, School of Public Health, University of North Carolina at Chapel Hill.

**Joseph S. Tulchin** is Professor of History and Director of the Office of International Programs, University of North Carolina at Chapel Hill.

**Cesar A. Vapnarsky** is Senior Researcher at the Centro de Estudios Urbanos y Regionales, Buenos Aires, Argentina.

# Introduction

JORGE ENRIQUE HARDOY

Poor housing and living conditions cause or contribute to most of the major health problems in the Third World. The lack of a healthy home and living environment is at the root of such widespread diseases as dysentery and infant diarrhea, typhoid, cholera, and tuberculosis. The incidence of these and many other diseases is determined, in part, by the house, its immediate surrounds, and the quality and/or availability of basic services such as a protected water supply and provision for the disposal of human and household wastes.

Medical research has built up an impressive fund of knowledge about individual diseases and the mechanisms by which they are transmitted. But relatively little work has been done on two crucial aspects of disease prevention and detection in the Third World: the connection between primary health care provision and programs to improve housing conditions, provide basic services, and complement health and hygiene education in the control of disease; and the necessity for professionals concerned with housing, building, and planning to see health as their major concern. Indeed, most professionals have little or no knowledge of the link between the housing environment the poor live in and the diseases that ravage their lives. Government housing programs often have little or no component for disease control. Usually, the standards for new housing are based on standards developed in Europe in the nineteenth or twentieth centuries in response to public health concerns prevalent in Europe at the time. These standards have little or no relevance to the needs, priorities, or major problems in most third world nations.

Most housing professionals and the government agencies they serve or advise have little knowledge of how a population already guards against health problems, what its needs and priorities are, how it feels concerning involvement in an initiative to improve health, and what it can afford in terms of time and payments to run and maintain new equipment or services. Unless a community has the knowledge and motivation, government and agency provision of resources may have little impact.

In designing an effective housing improvement or settlement strategy, there must be an understanding before program design of what action at what level will have the optimum impact. With a given amount of funds and human resources there is an inevitable trade off between the number of people who can be reached with some tangible improvement and the extent of the improvement. The need for some clear guidelines here is all the more important now that Third World governments and international agencies are increasingly thinking of giving more support to small rural towns and to rehabilitation/upgrading schemes in urban centers. A better knowledge of what the "beneficiaries" can actually afford and what the project costs is vital if we want to approach realistically any strategy based on the linkages between health and habitat.

If one steps back from housing policies and asks what is in fact their role, then the major reason for any publicly funded rural or urban housing program is to improve health and reduce the risk of disease. But current and past housing programs are not designed with this in mind. Indeed, the clearest evidence of the failure among housing professionals to see the relationship between habitat and health is the arbitrary way housing projects are designed, both by individual governments and by international agencies. No attempt is made to identify the major disease problems in the community for which the housing project is designed, nor is an attempt made to establish the health priorities of the community before designing the project.

Furthermore, there is little or no coordination between government housing programs and government health or education ministries or agencies. Yet housing programs, education programs (including adult education), and the provision of health care services and facilities are all necessary components of any realistic drive to improve housing and living conditions in the Third World. The funds that governments allocate to housing programs are still largely concentrated on financing the construction of subsidized public housing units and, more recently, "core" houses or "serviced sites" in the major cities (or city). The latter are built in such small numbers that they make little impact on the housing problem. (Slum and squatter upgrading programs have on occasion reached more families.) But rarely has there been a careful assessment of how an upgrading program can best improve health and control disease.

Thus, there is a clear need to improve the knowledge of housing, building, and planning professionals in the health aspects of housing projects and programs. There is also a need to encourage sectoral ministries and agencies within Third World nations and the specialized agencies within the United Nations system to coordinate efforts in this aspect of development planning. Furthermore, there is a need to clarify the direct links between disease and housing structure, plot location, a house's immediate environs, and services such as water supply and sanitation that are part of an "adequate" house.

Some changes in national and international response to health and habitat began to take place during the 1970s. The United Nations Conference on Human Settlements (Habitat) convened in Vancouver, Canada in May-June 1976 was a major event for governments and agencies because of the broad representation at the meeting and the enthusiastic consensus for the conference recommendations. Although many of the recommendations for national and international action adopted at Vancouver were postponed, the supply of safe drinking water and the institution of hygienic waste disposal were goals unanimously accepted. An action plan was outlined the following year at the United Nations Water Conference at Mar del Plata, Argentina that led to the International Drinking Water Supply and Sanitation Decade, 1981-1990. Few international cooperative efforts have had impact on as many people as the Water and Sanitation Decade. Although they fall short of initial objectives, the results have demonstrated the potential for success in efforts that combine a different attitude on the part of governments, lending, and technical assistance agencies when the components of a program are well defined and have concrete objectives. Inefficiencies and uncoordinated efforts continue to exist, but seldom have so many resources been mobilized to satisfy a basic human need. Perhaps as important is the interest shown by countries in strengthening the national capacity to plan, finance, execute, and evaluate what was accomplished.

After years of informal activities, several multilateral and bilateral agencies adopted formal health policies. The emphasis of the Interamerican Development Bank has been on lending for projects on potable water and sewers for urban areas, although rural health programs including the construction of health centers and the development of training programs have been implemented. The World Bank Group adopted a health policy in 1974 supplemented by policies in education, population, and nutrition. The World Bank Group, by far the largest lending agency in the world, also has emphasized water supply and sewerage projects, mostly for large urban areas, with a minor commitment to basic health and nutrition services, training information, and education activities. The same emphasis also was adopted by the Asian Development Bank, by the European Development Fund, and by smaller multilateral agencies.

UNICEF, through the promotion of primary health care and small-scale health programs, UNDP, United Nations Development Program, by assistance for improving health care, and the World Health Organization (WHO), through major disease control programs assistance to governments in developing national health plans, and improved project designs, and better health care management have been at the forefront of technical assistance for many years. However, resources are too small to finance the many field programs and manpower development programs that the developing countries require.

A major breakthrough at the international level might be taking place as a result of recent initiatives by the World Health Organization. WHO's general program of work (1984-1989) includes the promotion of environmental health with particular emphasis on rural and urban development housing. WHO has been concerned for many years about environmental health deficiencies in rural and urban areas. The causes of these deficiencies are complex, of enormous magnitude, and exacerbated by the poverty of many urban and rural dwellers, a shortage of resources, and the growing pressures of hundreds of millions of people living in completely inadequate conditions.

In 1984, the World Health Organization established the principles for a new program on the environmental health aspects of rural and urban development (RUD); these were based on the rationale that planned social and economic development offers the opportunity to improve health through a number of preventive environmental health measures. WHO acknowledged that constant changes in economic and social conditions make imperative the need for environmental health facilities and services to ameliorate hazards to health and/or to improve living conditions.

WHO and UNEP, United Nations Environmental Program, organized a technical panel to review and advise the planning and implementation of the WHO\UNEP project on the Environmental Health Aspect of Housing and Urban planning. The first meeting took place in Moscow in April 1985. The panel plans to hold biennial meetings. RUD has requested a number of reports: study and research for upgrading rural and urban settlements; preparation of environmental health criteria documents for human settlements, indoor climate, noise, the health impact of structural materials, etc; field studies on health effects and a collaborating center to compile and assess available information; training programs and principles and methods for environmental health planning and management. RUD's activities aim to foster national and international action so that by 1989 most countries will have undertaken environmental impact assessments in relation to both rural and urban development and housing and at least one-third of the countries should have developed policies and strategies to ensure that environmental health aspects are incorporated in rural and urban development and housing programs.

We are witnessing the beginning of activities that attempt to better comprehend the relationship between health, and physical well-being, and human habitat. Health policies of governments and international agencies show some interesting changes, although these changes are not as rapid as the urgent demands for social justice. After all, a vast majority of the Third World's population who live in poor and unhealthy conditions and are in poor health are not reached by any form of housing project or health program.

CHAPTER 1

# Habitat and Health: An Exploration of Their Interrelationship

JORGE ENRIQUE HARDOY

I would like to tackle the subject of health and habitat by using an analysis of housing, land, and human settlement policies carried out between 1977 and 1979 in seventeen Third World countries.[1] We encountered great difficulties in accurately evaluating the situation in these countries because of a lack of adequate social statistics.[2] Any attempt, therefore, to reach general conclusions would have been risky and devoid of relevance for those who believe themselves capable of designing policies based on other countries. Our study covered countries as dissimilar as Nepal and Mexico, Brazil and Iraq,[3] but certain similarities emerged. Inadequate and frequently misdirected government action was common to them all. In the year we carried out our fieldwork (1977-1978), none of the nations had an explicit and reasonably comprehensive policy with regard to human settlements. In virtually every one of them, most of the people were badly housed and were bereft of many basic services. Budgets for conventional housing construction alternative approaches and the provision of basic services were on too small a scale and had too low a priority in government planning. Politicians and planners gave preference to economic growth and postponed facing urgent social problems to some vague and unspecified time in the future.

I have also used other studies to elaborate this discussion. An investigation carried out in Southeast Asia in the early 1970s covered housing policies for low-income groups in Hong Kong, Singapore, Indonesia,

6

Malaysia, the Philippines, Sri Lanka, Thailand, and Laos.[4] The eight investigators present a more optimistic picture than that drawn by those who studied the seventeen countries mentioned above.[5] Another collection of reports on a number of cities in Latin America-- in Mexico, El Salvador, Paraguay, Colombia, and Venezuela--based on studies carried out in 1974 and 1976, shows very little cause for optimism.[6] I have also made use of monographs, theses, and research documents that have been discussed in recent years.[7] Finally, I have used an analysis of housing, land, and human settlement policies in twelve small countries in the Third World carried out between 1981 and early 1983.[8]

## SPONTANEOUS TRENDS IN POPULATION DISTRIBUTION

Between 1950 and 1980 the total population in Africa, Asia, and Latin America grew by an estimated 1.5 billion people. Another 1.6 billion will be added between 1980 and 2000; 60 percent of this population growth will be urban. During the last three decades, the bulk of this growth was concentrated in areas that had been settled for decades, centuries, or even millennia. Despite this phenomenal population growth, the occupation of areas that are or until recently have been unsettled or sparsely settled is still slow and largely unplanned. In addition, few new towns and cities have been designed or built in the already settled areas. The growing population is essentially finding space in already existing metropolises, cities, and towns, and in rural villages and areas. The combined population of the new cities started during the last thirty years represents only a small fraction of the Third World's annual population growth. The numbers involved in the spontaneous or planned occupation of new territories are still very modest, but they will inevitably grow and, depending on the way the growth is guided, it could promote or delay the economic development of those areas and of a country as a whole.

The displacement of a people to new territories with untapped land resources is prompted by:

(a) agrarian reforms, frequently complemented by colonization schemes. The unchallenged result of structural agrarian reforms was the incorporation of peasants and peasant communities as a formal official class. Before such agrarian reforms, peasants were alienated from civil societies and the state. When Mexico, Bolivia, and Cuba implemented their agrarian reforms, peasants felt that they had become an official class and, as such, they became a political force. This was not the case in countries where conventional marginal agrarian reforms were carried out, such as in Colombia, Ecuador, and Venezuela;

   (b)   the free displacement of people after independence, once colonial legislation forbidding migrations
was removed.  The creation of new national bureaucracies
attracted landless peasants and unskilled rural and
urban workers to the new national and regional centers;
   (c)   hunger and the endless struggle for survival
in already overcrowded and low-production rural areas.
Seen from another perspective, all or almost all Third
World cities are new cities.  In terms of size, population, diversity of functions, administration, local
institutions, economic base, and social problems, an agglomeration that grows from 4 to 16 million people or
from 1 to 4 million in a little more than a generation
should be called a new city.  No one has a clear idea of
how to tackle the city's growth and development problems
given the scarcity of public and private resources for
such tasks.  We can, however, detect some major trends
in the spontaneous redistribution of population in the
Third World: (a) a general trend towards urban areas in
all developing regions with marked concentration in the
larger centers in each country;(b) increasing density of
already settled agricultural areas, in many instances
reaching saturation in relation to present land tenancy
patterns and prevailing technologies; and (c)  the movement of still small numbers to new unsettled and sparsely settled territories.
   As Richardson points out, these dramatic changes
are the outcome of market forces.[9]   I would add that
these changes are taking place in a situation that shows
little room for optimism for the lower income groups.
Underemployment for unskilled workers is increasing and
income distribution in most developing countries is
deteriorating for the lower income groups.   Given the
numbers involved, fewer and fewer countries will be able
to provide for the basic needs of their people unless a
drastic change in the world's priorities takes place.
If these assumptions are correct, then we should expect
a general deterioration in the human habitat of most developing countries with different and unforeseeable impact on health and, as a result, on the future development of these countries.


**RURAL HOUSING**

In the majority of the countries in both our seventeen-
and twelve-country analyses, governments had no programs
for building or improving rural housing.   Information
concerning other countries reveals a similar situation.
Census data on housing conditions in rural areas, when
available, is too general and aggregated and therefore
of little use for policymakers and specialists. Some
housing projects have been or are being carried out in
official agricultural settlements or in integrated agri-

cultural development programs. In such projects, the smallest share of the funds goes to investment in welfare, housing, and education. The bulk of the money is earmarked for new production units, the development of marketing facilities, and training of the work force.

The private sector invests very little in rural housing. When it does so, its objective is to house administrative or technical personnel and the skilled work force who live in the hamlets that spring up around plantations. Rural housing is consequently the responsibility of the people who live there. They build with local materials in accordance with very old traditional designs and techniques and with the help of their families and sometimes the community.

Although every rural family has some sort of housing, a high percentage live in very poor and overcrowded conditions. Accurate estimates are difficult to find because few rural censuses are taken, and when they are, the data are presented in an aggregated form. Poor rural housing, exemplified by overcrowding and poor ventilation, with no access to piped water, and built so as to give little protection from insects that spread disease, is one of the principal causes of the high mortality rate, in particular infant mortality, in rural areas. If a piped water supply existed, cholera, dysentery, and infantile diarrhea could decrease sharply. If traditional building materials were treated and insect screens installed in the houses, the incidence of malaria and other diseases spread by insects could be curbed. If latrines were installed, schistosomiasis and other debilitating sicknesses transmitted by worms could be more effectively controlled. Tuberculosis could be reduced by better nourishment, as well as by less overcrowding and improved ventilation in the dwellings. All these are diseases of unhealthy living conditions rooted in poverty and illiteracy and aggravated by malnutrition. Unfortunately, most studies on poverty in the Third World are of a descriptive nature without identifying its causes.

Many diseases closely associated with the social and economic characteristics of man's made habitat affect hundreds of millions of people and cause the death of millions of human beings annually. "All of these social and economic factors have rarely been incorporated in the planning of disease control efforts, thus leading to activities which may have been inappropriate and unacceptable to the people at risk or infested."[10] The physical and mental debility they cause prevents millions from effectively joining the work force or drastically curtails their productive capacity. The diseases, which are generally considered to be the cause of the debility of the rural population, are beginning to form part of the urban sanitation problem as well, partly due to the accelerating deterioration of the urban habitat and partly because they are brought in by rural migrants.[11]

Few developing countries have given serious thought to the problems of the rural habitat, despite the fact that in most Asian and African countries and in some of the smallest Latin American countries the rural population will continue to increase rapidly, at least for the next generation. In some of these countries--e.g., India, Bangladesh, and Pakistan--there is already insufficient rural land to provide adequate livelihood for the present rural population. In many others, among them Haiti, El Salvador, the countries of the Sahel, some East African and Andean countries, and a number of Arab countries, adequate absorption of the rural population could be brought about only by drastic land reforms and prudent investment in activities that would permit increased productivity of arid, semi-desert and/or badly eroded land. Without economic improvement in the rural areas, it is practically impossible to envisage positive changes in the rural habitat.

Among the seventeen nations covered by our work, very few showed any concern for the rural habitat. In Indonesia, building information centers have been set up, and some village development programs have been formulated that include housing improvement. No major housing programs exist in Egypt, Iraq, Jordan, the Sudan, Nigeria, Colombia, Brazil, or Bolivia. In Tanzania, the Housing Bank extended its loan facilities to rural areas with the intention of funding 32,000 permanent dwellings in rural villages up to 1981. The Tunisian Development Plan (1977-1981) envisaged the construction of 40,000 rural dwellings, a figure that represented half the publicly funded housing planned for that period. In India, a program has been in place for years to provide landless laborers with plots to build their dwellings on; this had produced 5.8 million plots by the end of 1975. The rural housing program of Kerala State in India, initiated in the early 1970s, was based on the mobilization of local groups and gave preference to landless families. Kenya has concentrated its efforts on equipping rural villages with basic services. In Malaysia, the approach changed in favor of constructing new villages. In Thailand, a program relocating urban inhabitants to rural areas was started. How significant are these programs? Of what worth are these national development plans with their declared commitment to rural housing? What difference do some few hundred thousand conventional rural dwellings make, newly built or rehabilitated with public sector money, and spread over all the countries of the Third World-- when the rural population grows at an average annual rate of 25 million people?

I do not share the point of view of those who look optimistically at the situation because governments show

greater concern for rural housing in their documents or
because some projects are going ahead and a few special
agencies are set up.  Nor can I agree with those who
maintain that the standard of rural housing is higher
than that of urban housing.  What is such a comparison
meant to indicate?  Is it not, perhaps, a pretext for
concentrating investment of the insufficient resources
allocated by governments and agencies to housing in the
urban centers?  What criteria are used to compare the
quality of rural and urban housing? Is urban overcrowding not, perhaps, connected with the lack of opportunity, exploitation, and poor living conditions of the
farm laborer?  Wherever any kind of rural productive
activity exists, be it a plantation, a farm, a large or
a small estate, there will be some sort of housing:
isolated dwellings or a settlement, a rural hamlet established at random, or a small country town.  The quality and variety of available services will vary in accordance with the production potential, the tenancy
system, and the political strengths of the interests
rooted in the area.

One additional factor in the rural habitat, that
seldom is taken into account. . . .the migrants and the
group formed by "professional migrants," to use Feder's
term.[12]   Both groups include tens of millions of
landless peasants and underemployed rural workers every
year.  Their living conditions are, as a rule, the worst
one can find and undoubtedly pose health problems of a
magnitude that has not yet been fully determined. Obviously, colonization schemes are not an answer, given
their numbers, to the needs of these groups.

Summing up, I don't know of any study that has systematically tried to assess the few examples of official
rural housing programs.  The scanty data collected in
our analyses and from reports of multilateral agencies
show that the new settlement areas, irrigation areas,
and areas of commercial cultivation where displaced
people are relocated are almost exclusively favored
areas.  Most rural people continue to build their simple
dwellings by their own efforts, with local materials,
siting them where the tenancy system and their own
requirements lead them, completely alien to official
norms, criteria, and support.


**URBAN HOUSING**

Third World cities are becoming increasingly alike.
Neither topography, climate, building materials, nor
cultural and ecological differences are sufficient in
many cases to tell one from another. Beset by very similar problems--demographic pressures, speculative interests, class structures, technological uniformity,
weak local governments, economic imperatives, and inade-

quate investment for construction and administration--
Third World cities present an aspect of increasing
sameness and decay.  Only older sections and historic
centers retain the cultural characteristics that distinguish one region, culture, or religion from another.
The modern cities sprawl.  They grow without limits,
without giving thought to their future, and without any
worries on the part of the decision makers about the
social cost of uncontrolled expansion. Nobody thinks of
the city as a city.  Very few of the inhabitants of a
big city think of themselves as citizens.  For those who
have money and live in residential suburbs or areas well
away from the center, the streets are nothing other than
ways and means of daily travel.  For those who have no
money and live in poverty-stricken shantytowns located
on any empty site in degrading circumstances, there is
no street, no square, no feature in their immediate surroundings that could claim their interest or loyalty.

Nobody seems to have a clear idea of how to meet
"the colossal financial and administrative needs of
rapid urbanization."[13]  At least nobody with the power
to make decisions has any clear idea of how to create a
humanized environment.  The official structure of a
class-segregated city is accepted. Neighborhoods that
boast buildings constructed with the most eccentric,
uneconomic, pseudo-aesthetic materials imaginable, rub
shoulders with areas of the most abject poverty.
Nowhere is the contrast between poor and rich, between
power and impotence, shown more strikingly than in the
neighborhoods and buildings of a modern city.

No country of the Third World, with the possible
exception of Singapore, officially builds the required
number of housing units.  In practically all countries,
nonofficial building overtakes the public sector program
to the extent that, in some cases, nine out of ten dwellings added to the national housing stock each year are
privately and unofficially built.  Of course, the quality of nonofficial building is not subject to control,
with the result that these countries are increasingly
faced with a quality imbalance and varying shortfalls in
the ratio of housing units to inhabitants.  Governments
frequently make optimistic statements based on the
assumption that the high economic growth rates that many
Third World countries achieved in the 1960s and early
1970s would enable them to launch official housing programs for low-income groups. Unfortunately, these statements are not matched by reality.

We do not need detailed studies to link poverty
with the quality of housing.  For much of the Third
World's urban and rural population, poverty is a chronic
condition. There are many illiterates and undernourished
children and adults who are not able to satisfy their
basic survival needs or who do not have access to

services. For this reason, a totally new approach to housing is needed.

## Housing the Lower Classes in Urban Areas

To meet their housing needs, the urban poor occupy land or buy a plot in an often illegally subdivided area where they construct a dwelling by their own efforts with the help of family and friends. Or they rent a room in a common lodging house or a hostel, or rent a hut or a shack they may eventually buy in a shantytown. The former contributes to the horizontal growth of a city. The latter leads to over-crowding until the absorptive capacity of the common lodging house or the shantytown has reached the saturation point, and it is no longer possible to squeeze in newcomers. Many poor also live in the servants' quarters in the upper class houses where they work.

Few poor people manage to secure accommodation in a public project. Even with low-interest public loans, very few are able to buy homes. Usually they do not earn sufficient money to pay the loan installments because they have no regular employment or they do not belong to officially recognized organizations or trade unions. Although the means for acquiring accommodation differ from one country to another and among regions and cities of the same country, some generalizations can be made. The percentage of people living in slums is usually highest in the large metropolitan areas--in cities where the population is increasing rapidly due to intensive public and private sector investment--and sometimes in rural settlements around plantations or areas of commercial farming, as well as in medium-sized or small towns. The number of people who live in common lodging houses, boarding houses, or servants' quarters is generally insignificant in medium-sized and small centers, but is greater in the big metropolitan areas, in particular those that have been urbanized for some time. Houses built by the owners themselves in illegal urban developments represent a comparatively high percentage in the big metropolitan areas of each country. However, the lack of basic services and community facilities render the fairly general insecurity of housing in smaller towns and villages more acute.

Living conditions in the dwellings built by the people's own efforts in shantytowns and clandestine squatters' camps have often been improved with the passage of time. The impression of researchers and census results confirms that a gradual change for the better has taken place. For instance, there is a greater use of permanent building materials for walls, roofs, and, to a lesser extent, floors, more incorporation of latrines and more spacious accommodation. There is also an increase in the number of units supplied with water piped either directly to the unit or to the

neighborhood and the population has greater access to
certain educational and health services in some quarters.  I do not know of systematic studies of whether
these improvements, achieved without public subsidy,
compensate for the evident deterioration of the habitat.
It is my impression that, on balance, nonpublic sector,
lower class housing in the developing countries is
deteriorating and that the improved quality of life
found in a few quarters does not stem the formation of
new shantytowns, the increase of illegal situations, or
the general deterioration of the immediate environment.

Where are these forms of lower class housing
located?  The great majority of common lodging houses or
hostels are found in city centers and are connected to
the services of those districts.  Some are in neigh-
'borhoods somewhat further away that were small population centers and are now physically incorporated into
the metropolitan area.  The building of common lodging
houses was originally legal and was one of the two
initial forms of lower class housing.  Some common lodging houses, still in use, are more than one hundred
years old. The tenants generally pay a low rent. In many
countries, unamended rent acts have frozen the rents, so
that the landlords have given up carrying out
maintenance and repairs.  Government authorities are not
eager to take decisive action such as appropriating the
lodging houses with little or no compensation and using
the rent and other resources for their rehabilitation.
The building of new common lodging houses or the conversion of large old houses into common lodging houses
is illegal in many countries.  However, the conversion
of large old buildings in the old city centers and even
in outlying areas, with the object of maximizing income
from properties situated in rundown districts, continues
without control.

Boarding houses and residential hotels or family
hotels are variants of the lodging houses. But the con-
tractual relationships between proprietors and tenants
are different and are not subject to rent laws in the
same way.  They began as temporary residences for more
affluent persons.  Originally built to a higher standard, overcrowding, a low standard of sanitary facilities, the use of the rooms for cooking, and general
decay cause the buildings to deteriorate.  In some
metropolitan areas of Argentina, Uruguay, and Chile,
they make up a significant percentage of urban accommodation.

Shantytowns are the most common habitat of the
lower classes in Third World cities.  They developed as
squatters encroached on empty public or private land on
the outskirts or the central sections of the city like
the port of Buenos Aires, the banks of the Rimac River
in Lima, near the old ramparts in San Juan in Puerto
Rico, or on railway tracks no longer in use.  As central

sites filled up and controls increased, the incursions were directed to sites ever further from the center, although proximity to the central city also led to the occupation of unsuitable sites, such as the hills of Rio de Janeiro and La Paz, the gorges in Guatemala and San Salvador, the dry bed of the lake in Mexico City, and so on.  In other words, the location of shantytowns depends on availability of space, accessibility to sources of income, and proximity to basic services (especially water and transport).

The situation of the inhabitants is unsettled. They illegally occupy land that has, also illegally, been used for housing.  In spite of this, there exist active secondary markets in all shantytowns for selling, letting, or subletting units at prices that are sometimes quite high.  The quality of the housing is usually abysmal.  The services are used collectively, although there may be clandestine connections to piped water and electricity lines.  As the shantytowns become consolidated, the authorities provide a few social amenities.  Government action toward shantytowns varies greatly, although it is possible to find clear corre-lations between types of government and the housing po-licies.  These policies range from forcible expulsion of shantytown inhabitants to acknowledgement of their exis-tence and halfhearted attempts at rehabilitation; from experiments in eradication and relocation to supply of some community services, partial settlement legaliza-tion and improvement projects.

Governments in the developing countries are begin-ning to accept that squatter settlements and other illegal alternatives to basic shelter and services are inevitable.  Although some governments have started to do something about this situation, more often than not they do not recognize occupancy or tenure, (which would be the first step), nor do they permit and encourage community groups to participate in the discussion of renovation plans, norms, or project implementation.  In recent years, some governments have initiated more con-crete housing measures.  The improvement of shantytowns, shacks, or sections invaded by squatters was given priority over public sector projects for new sites and services or projects financed by multilateral or bi-lateral agencies.  The obvious reason for these policy changes was that the cost of improving a dwelling in a shantytown was  less than the cost of installing a site with services. Moreover, in this way, the existing social organization was not destroyed.

A last form of access for the poor to housing must be mentioned:  organized illegal urban settlements, an alternative much used in the cities of Colombia, Mexico, and El Salvador, among others.  They are located at the periphery of the big cities and respect neither the laws of the country nor of the city. In many cases, the

original occupants have transferred the occupancy of the
land illegally, although usually the plot was sold to
the developers in a legal manner. Generally speaking,
the developers do not present plans for approval to the
responsible authorities. The type of housing is the
family unit, of greatly varying quality. Some houses are
much the same as shantytown shacks; others are built
predominantly with industrial materials.

. ## Public Sector Housing

Official housing projects embarked on by public
agencies with or without outside funding tend to be
located where a number of criteria are met: availability of suitable public land; availability of suitable
private land at a price compatible with the project's
objectives; existence of streets or approach roads in
the neighborhood to facilitate the mobility of the future inhabitants; and existence of basic amenities
(piped water, electricity, and, depending on the planned
density, sewers) close to the site of the project.
Proximity and/or easy access to sources of income and to
community services (e.g., schools and clinics) is a factor which should also be taken into account when siting
a housing project, but rarely is.

A decent house is universally acknowledged as
essential for improving the health of a population, for
raising labor productivity, for reducing the cost of
health programs, for consolidating family unity, and for
raising the spirit of a population. The quality of housing is regarded as a significant sign of the
socioeconomic progress of a country. A housing program,
humble as it may be, adds significantly to the capital
formation of a country, contributing directly to the
creation of employment in the building industry and indirectly in related industries and activities. An
appropriate housing program should also be regarded as a
redistributive policy, humble as it also may be. In
most developing countries, the construction and related
industries are potentially the major sources after agriculture of immediate unskilled employment. Furthermore,
housing is considered one of the basic rights of all
human beings, one of the prerequisites for physical
survival.

Concepts such as these are included in almost all
national development plans, in the platforms of political parties, in the programs of governments, in the
publications of national and international agencies, and
in the documents approved at international congresses.
However, such apparent goodwill is not matched by
reality. Few governments have seriously and realistically considered urban housing programs that meet the
needs of a burgeoning population. Housing programs
rarely address the permanent changes in spatial distribution that result from population growth nor do they

seek to overcome existing deficits or replace obsolete
stock. Realistic housing standards and urban norms that
reconcile different environments, cultural patterns,
family size, economic resources, and the available na-
tional/regional capital are missing in all regions. The
major cause of the failure of public housing projects
around the world is the lack of participation of those
for whom the programs and projects are intended.

Governments have chosen to adopt conventional housing programs even if implicitly they accept that through
this approach the bottom 30, 40, or 60 percent of the
urban population will never have access to adequate
shelter. In developing countries, conventional housing,
inexpensive as it may seem to the people in developed
countries, means subsidized housing, generally intended
for public employees, the armed forces, members of the
official unions, or the inhabitants of an urban area
that the government wants to promote for political or
economic reasons. But subsidies, when they cannot be
spread to all members of the population, are discrimina-
tory and favor the official sectors of society over the
informal sectors, the "legal" members of society over
the "illegal."

Two parallel cities are clearly emerging side by
side in all developing countries: the city inhabited by
those who can pay for goods and services, including
housing, and the city of those who can scarcely afford
the minimum goods and have practically no access to any
services. We could call them the legal and the illegal
city, the official and the unofficial city. Both cities
need each other, one cannot survive without the other.
A newspaper ad by the Congress Party appeared in Delhi
in January 1983 and included the following text: "Delhi
is not just another city. It is India's key city.
India's capital. India's proud capital. And Delhi has
reason to be proud. Compare its roads with those of the
finest cities in the world and Delhi emerges an
equal."[14] The ad went on to praise the 332 kilometers
of new roads and the 7 overpasses the United Party had
built recently, and the 96 new kilometers of roads, the
5 overpasses, and large bridge over the Yamina river
that were planned. But one doesn't have to travel very
far to witness the other side of the coin--the illegal
city where the very poor dwell, work, care for their
health, and struggle to survive.

In the foreseeable future, cities will still be
built by means of an immense variety of individual
efforts coordinated at family or family-plus-friends
levels. Such an approach to the construction of urban
environments is not new. In present times as well as in
the past, self-built urban environments have been the
principal habitat for the urban poor. In the cities of
the past and in today's cities, the bulk of the housing
stock and many services were and are built by individual

efforts. What is new is the size of these efforts. We cannot grasp the enormous variety of problems and decisions involved in the self-construction of urban environments, but I think we are learning to understand what is involved in these processes. Self-built urban environments exhibit great diversities. However, some things seem to be common to most of them: (a) they show an intense use of the site and of the dwelling space, which are often used for other activities; and (b) they are associated with informal activities, with the organic use of the plot layout, and with the use of local and/or discarded building materials.

## THE HEALTH AND HOUSING LINK

Reducing poverty and improving nutritional levels, both in rural and urban areas, is the first step to better health because most of the critical health problems of the poor are rooted in poverty. But "absolute poverty is not likely to be eliminated by the year 2000," recognizes the World Bank in its 1982 Annual Report. Oscar Altimir states that "at the beginning of the seventies, 40 percent of Latin American households were poor, which included 26 percent of the urban households and 60 percent of the rural households."[15] Twenty percent of the households in Latin America were classified as destitute ten years ago. The percentages of poor and destitute are higher in Africa and Asia. But where are the poorest located, and how do we comparatively measure poverty in each continent and in each nation? It is clear that the poor are located on the periphery of most large agglomerations and in the less developed rural areas.

Famines, the starkest examples of malnutrition, are better checked these days. Since they are geographically localized, it has been possible to provide aid. But chronic malnutrition remains the crucial contemporary social problem, and its cause is not any physical limit to food producing but the political constraints on distribution.[16] As long as this remains true, there will be severe constraints on our ability to improve the health of the world's poor. Although most of the best lands in the Third World are under cultivation, especially in Asia, lands that could potentially be cultivated represent 36 percent of the total surface of Latin America, 23 percent in Asia, and 24 percent in Africa. According to the Food and Agriculture Organization (FAO), present food production is sufficient to satisfy the basic needs of the world's population. Only 43 percent of the potentially cultivable land is under cultivation, and present yields are well below those theoretically possible. The cultivation of new lands could be increased by the colonization of new areas, but

at a higher cost per unit of production than the cultivation of the best and better located lands. Naturally,
the exploitation of the new land will depend on the
economic resources available in each national entity.[17]
There is also another urgent consideration--the degradation of lands that are presently under cultivation and
threatened by erosion, reduction in soil fertility, and
urban sprawl.

If, as previously mentioned, there are no physical
limits to the production of food for the present world's
population and for the population foreseen in the immediate future, it would seem logical to expect that there
should be no material limits either to the production of
viable human habitats if different societies improve
already prevailing technologies and adapt them to the
availability of the raw materials and human skills in
each region. In each region, however, there are social
and political constraints of different kinds. The
economic and productive structure and the resources in
each region and country have limitations that can be an-
ticipated and that constitute important obstacles to
habitat programs. Much improvement in the living conditions of the masses of the poor and in their working
potentials could be achieved with simple solutions that
are not beyond the human, technical, and financial
possibilities of many Third World nations, or at least,
they are not beyond the world's possibilities.

The object of public intervention in housing,
whether in large cities, towns, or rural areas, is to
ensure that a group of people obtain some mix of the
following elements: more secure tenure, better protection from natural elements (weather, floods, earthquakes, etc.); more room; access to safe drinking water;
more hygienic and more convenient disposal of household
and human wastes; access to cheap building materials;
and access to job or income opportunities. The purpose
of public intervention is also to provide some mix of
these elements at a price the target group can afford
that does not involve a high unit subsidy. High subsidies limit the number of people an initiative can
reach. Although most of these interventions are not ex-
plicitly related to health, every one of them, directly
or indirectly, has a bearing on health since it has a
bearing on one or more of the physical, social,
economic, or environmental factors that affect health.

Yet, in the design of most housing projects or
programs, the relationship between habitat and health is
not recognized or understood by the housing/settlement
specialists who are in a position to make this relationship explicit. No attempt is made to identify either
the major health problems in the targeted community or
those groups most vulnerable to health problems whose
needs deserve special attention. No attempt is made to
establish the health priorities of that community before

project design begins. Perhaps too little thought is given to the trade-off between the number of people the program intends to reach and its impact on each individual or household.

Thus, although medical research has extensive knowledge about individual diseases and the mechanisms by which they are transmitted, there are four areas related to the physical environment that remain little-understood by housing and settlement professionals and agencies. The first is knowledge of the links between the physical environment of the targeted community and the health hazards its inhabitants have to cope with. Public housing programs or serviced-site schemes, or even slum and shantytown upgrading projects, often do not have a component directly focused on health problems since health problems were not identified prior to project design. Of course there is the hope that improved water supplies and/or improved disposal of household and human wastes might have some effect on health. But the decision as to what components the project includes is not based on the correlation between habitat and improved health. Official building standards, or the codes and norms used in infrastructure and service provision whose essential purpose is safety and health, bear little resemblance to the needs, priorities, and major health problems found in most Third World nations. Building codes are still based on those developed in Europe in the late nineteenth and early twentieth centuries in response to public health and safety concerns current then. Yet even when attempts have been made to adopt more realistic and more appropriate building codes or building material standards, or where, at project level (say in a serviced-site scheme), official building regulations are ignored, the standards are still not designed to respond directly to the health needs, priorities, and resources of the targeted community. Similarly, the norms used and accepted by national government and by foreign consultants for infrastructure and service provision are also often overdesigned so that costs per serviced house rise and limit the potential impact of the investment, and the possibility of cost recovery.

The second area that's barely understood is how improvements to the physical environment have to interact with social, economic, and environmental aspects if any initiative to improve housing and living conditions is to be fully effective. The literature on health or housing projects is full of stories where public intervention failed because it neglected one or more environmental factor that contributed to the community's poor health. For instance, a new water supply meant to enable households to use more water is not accompanied by provision for the disposal of waste water thus water collects in pools in and around the settlement and

provides breeding grounds for mosquitoes carrying malaria, filariasis, or other diseases. The installation of
efficient and hygienic latrines for the purpose of de-
creasing the incidence of schistosomiasis does not deal
with (say) the problem of children bathing in snail-
infested ponds, and thereby greatly diminishes the effect of the investment in latrines. Likewise, the health
impact of well-designed and maintained latrines is
greatly decreased when attention is not paid to the
transmission of fecal-oral diseases other than by waterborne vectors--for instance, by inadequate washing and
bathing.

Then there is the problem of cost recovery and
"affordability." Reports of many housing projects, including squatter resettlement projects, subsidized public housing units, and even some serviced-site schemes,
demonstrate that some or indeed most of the "beneficiaries" were actually worse off. Although the physical
environment was improved, the improvement was negated by
the increase in cost to the beneficiaries. They either
had to pay more than they could afford, or the move from
their old house to the new one meant a loss in income
(perhaps because of increased transport costs to work or
perhaps because of decreased income-earning opportunities for secondary-income earners in the new settlements).

The third area of weakness is knowledge of how the
population already guards against health problems, what
its priorities and needs are, how it feels it would like
to be involved in an initiative to improve health, and
what it can afford in terms of time and payments to run
and maintain new equipment or services. For some outside
agency simply to install a new water supply is not
enough if people still use contaminated water. Perhaps
the new water source is not so conveniently located, or
perhaps it has a strange taste to those not used to it.
They do not understand the link between, say, the common
fecal-oral diseases they experience and the traditional
sources of water. Or perhaps the payments required for
the new piped water are too expensive for many households. Unless the community has the knowledge and motivation, just providing the resources will have little
impact. A project to supply protected water has to have
built into it an understanding that this water must be
conveniently located for all households. There must be
sufficient community involvement in the project's design, implementation, maintenance, and, where appropriate, cost recovery to ensure the protected water will be
fully used and kept uncontaminated. If insufficient attention is paid to maintenance, then the new water
source may even increase the incidence of waterborne
diseases, because, once contaminated, it acts as a centralized source of infection. Built into an understanding of community needs and priorities should be an

awareness that the community itself may have evolved
some quite rational and cheap responses to disease control.  In certain instances, a failure to understand
these has severely limited the effect of public intervention on health.  For instance, in Africa, many settlements were set back traditionally from fast flowing
rivers. New settlement programs promoted by governments
forced people to settle beside these rivers, only to
discover that the reason the original settlements were
at some distance from these was to guard against river-
blindness caused by flies that bred on the banks of the
rivers.

The final area of weak knowledge is in the understanding of what action at what level will have the
optimum impact (see Figure 1.1).  With a given amount of
funds and human resources, there is an inevitable trade-
off between the number of people who can be reached with
some tangible improvement and the extent of that
improvement.  In designing housing improvement or settlement strategies, there is little attention given to
what will have the most effect:  for instance, whether
to concentrate on water supply to each house, sewage
connections, and garbage disposal, or protected wells;
whether to mount a public campaign to teach adults and
children personal hygiene or construct pit latrines.
Indeed, in the whole area of "public action" in small
towns and rural areas, there is very little idea as to
what action at what level can do the most to improve
housing and living conditions.  The need for some clear
guidelines here is all the more important now that Third
World governments are thinking increasingly of giving
more support to agricultural development, rural housing
programs, and "integrated rural development" strategies.
Already certain governments have repeated in rural
housing programs the mistakes they made in urban areas
in constructing heavily subsidized housing units.  Often
the houses so constructed are not popular with the
intended beneficiaries because their design neglects
traditional climatic modification techniques common to
virtually all traditional housing.  The gap between what
the "beneficiaries" can actually afford and what the
housing costs is even higher than in cities, since most
rural livelihood comes from cultivation of subsistence
crops, cash income in rural areas is very low. Thus,
governments construct relatively few units at a high
cost, to which only a tiny portion of the rural population has access.  And since the major health problems
probably relate more to inadequate education, contaminated water supplies, lack of income or land, and no access to primary health care, these "rural housing"
programs have little beneficial effect and a very low
return when assessed by any comprehensive cost-benefit
analysis.

There is a need to clarify how the work of housing/settlement professionals and agencies should interact with the people their work is meant to benefit, with professionals from other disciplines, and with the staff from other agencies whose work also relates to or impinges on "health." There is a clear need to clarify the major health problems that relate directly or indirectly to "housing" in the widest sense--structure, plot, surrounds, basic services like water supply, sanitation, and garbage disposal. There is a need, too, for other specialists--for instance, community workers-- to appreciate the links between housing and health, and for health and educational specialists to see the link in their work with housing/settlement specialists. Then, finally, there is a need to encourage much stronger coordination between professionals working in different disciplines and agencies so that each better understands his or her role in a broad development strategy to improve the health of the poor.

**FUTURE TRENDS**

Some aspects of health and housing must be taken into account from the start of any program design, and they deserve careful analysis. These include: the conflict in most government plans between what can really be done and what is finally done; the insignificant impact made by existing programs on the unchecked deterioration in both urban and rural areas of most countries; the gulf between official programs and the priorities of the people; and the root causes of the current situation.
What can people expect from their governments? Such levels of incompetence have been reached that it is difficult to keep hoping that something positive will happen. As basic planning objectives, governments subscribe to a redistributive policy and then fail to fulfill their promises--scores of recommendations were adopted in Vancouver (United Nations Conference on Habitat, June 1976) that were promptly forgotten afterward. Governments decide on a housing program that is the first to go by the board when other priorities require funding. Governments, after years of shilly-shallying, finally formulate a program and do it badly. Can we, therefore, be surprised that government is frequently accused of arrogance and hypocrisy?
Let us start with some concrete facts. Few governments in developing countries are truly interested in the problem of human settlements. The way people live, their habitat, like so many other social problems, just does not excite world interest.[18] Is this due to ignorance, or is it that these problems are considered less urgent than those that capture world attention, such as energy, the environment, international trade,

FIGURE 1.1  Action Improving Physical Environment
(Some Health Problems and Needed Public Action at Different Levels)

| Health Problem | Action at House and Surroundings | Action at Neighborhood or Community/Village Level |
|---|---|---|
| Contaminated water--typhoid, hepatitis, cholera, dysenteries, diarrhea, guinea worm, etc. | Protected water supply to house; hygienic water storage within house. | Provision of supply infrastructure for this. Knowledge and motivation in community to use it. |
| Human waste disposal--potential for this to contaminate water/food or come into contact with human/disease vectors. | Adequately designed and maintained latrines, septic tanks or sewage connections. | Needed mix of technical advice, installation equipment and its servicing and maintenance (mix dependent on technology used). |
| Disposal of waste water and garbage--to get rid of stagnant pools and household wastes which attract disease/ disease vectors. | Adequate provision for drainage of waste water and provision for space to store garbage safely (e.g., dog/rat-proof stores). | Provision for drainage infrastructure. |
| Disease related to inadequate personal hygiene and lack of washing facilities--trachoma, skin and fecal-oral diseases. | Adequate water supply for washing and bathing. Provision for laundry either at house or community level. | Health and personal hygiene education for children and adults. Perhaps laundry facilities, if not in houses. |
| Disease vectors or parasites living in house structure with access to occupants/ food/water, e.g., rodents, vectors for Chagas disease and leithmaniasis. | Support for improved house structure (e.g., tiled floors, protected food storage areas, roofs-walls-floors protected against disease vectors. | Technical advice and information; part of adult and educational program. |
| Overcrowding, inadequate size structure--respiratory diseases, stress, household accidents, etc. | Technical and financial support for house improvement or extension. | Technical advice on improved ventilation; education on over-crowding-related diseases and accidents; recreation and play space provision. |
| No access to curative/ preventative health care/ advice. | Availability of simple primer for households on first aid/ health. | Primary health care center and easy availability to health-related goods. |
| House sites subject to landslides/floods as result of no other land being available for poorer groups. | Regularize tenure if dangers can be lessened and basic service provision; otherwise, offer alternative site. | Action to reduce dangers and encourage upgrading or offer alternative sites. |
| Illegal occupation of site or illegal subdivision with disincentive to upgrade and lack of services. | Steps to regularize tenure and provide basic services. | Work with community in providing basic infrastructure and services and incorporating it into "official" city. |
| Nutritional deficiencies and lack of income. | Preventative action to reduce work burden. Support for income generating activities within house. | Ensure availability of vegetable plots? Food/vitamin supplements? Support for commercial/industrial operations. |

| Action at Settlement or District Level | Action at National Level |
|---|---|
| Plans to undertake this and resources to do so. | |
| Plans to undertake this plus resources. Manpower and financial base to service and maintain. | Ensure that local government units have the financial and technical base to undertake these. Also that official norms and standards used in all infra-structure are appropriate to needs and to the resources available. |
| Regular removal or provision for safe disposal of household wastes and plans plus resources for drainage. | |
| Support for this. | Technical and financial resources to support such educational campaigns. Coordination of housing, health and education ministries/agencies in this. |
| Support for this through loans for upgrading house and ensure needed materials are cheap and easily available. | Ensure building codes and official procedures for approving house construction or improvement are not inhibiting this. Support for nationwide avail-ability of building loans, cheap materials (where possible based on local resources) and perhaps building advice centers. Production of technical and educational material to support this. |
| Support for this through loans (in-cluding small ones with flexible re-payment), building advice centers, etc. | |
| Small hospital and resources to sup-port lower level centers. | Technical/financial support for nationwide system of hospitals, health care centers, dispensaries, etc., and nationwide availability of needed drugs and health-related goods. Production of primer. |
| Ensure availability of safe housing sites that lower income groups can afford. | National legislation plus financial and technical support for local and city governments' inter-vention in land market--to ensure this is possible. Training institutions to provide needed manpower for all levels. |
| Support for this. | |
| Ensure space is left for vegetable plots and for commercial/industrial enterprises in settlements. | Structural reforms and other measures to improve poor's economic base. |

industrialization, population growth, and participation
in technological advancement? Or is it because the
problem is so vast that nobody knows how to tackle it?
Governments attempt to do something about settlements
without doing anything about society as a whole. They
treat settlements as an isolated factor, when nothing
could be further from the truth.

Of what benefit will the present, sketchy strategies for urban growth be? Who will be living in those
satellite or twin towns, in districts refashioned in an
urban pattern, or in those cities within cities? If we
project the growth of metropolitan areas twenty-five
years ahead and look at the recent experience in both
urban and rural districts, we come to the conclusion
that there will be no great improvement in the supply of
housing to the classes of the population with a low or
nonexistent capacity for savings, i.e., for families
whose income is below $2,500 per annum (US$ 500 per
person, per annum). This segment of the population may
well account for 60 percent of the families in Third
World countries. We can expect improved access to piped
water, and we can expect a little more of everything
that has been done so far: (a) sites and services, projects and improvements to informal and formal housing
for the middle – income groups, some with adequate
communal amenities and others almost without amenities;
(b) expansion of piped water systems, main sewers,
electricity, and transport networks, starting in the
sections legally incorporated in the cities with some
extensions to some outlying sections; (c) public credit
for the middle-income and private credit for the high-
income sectors; (d) emphasis on technologies with high
energy consumption for the mass production of the materials used, and, of course, inevitably, for the ele-
vators and air-conditioning for the apartment houses,
shops, and offices; (e) priority given to individual
transport over mass transportation as in the building of
highways; and (f) feeble attempts at controlling the
increase in land values and at conserving the natural
environment.

Public sector investment will continue to favor
urban areas to the detriment of the countryside, and the
great metropolitan concentrations to the disadvantage of
medium and small towns. Centralization will become more
pronounced in both decisionmaking and program control.
Local government will continue to lose economic and political power, except, sometimes, for the municipalities of federal districts in some national capitals.
The voice of the people and related movements and institutions will be heard less and less in decisionmaking.

The spontaneous movement of people to urban areas
that are unprepared to receive tens or hundreds of
thousands of new dwellers every year poses growing problems that no national or local administration is at-

tempting to control. Crowding already is and inevitably will be one of the major problems. Children, especially, who bear the brunt of the displacement from rural to urban areas, are more likely to catch certain diseases, such as measles, earlier in their lives and with fewer defenses. Many of the diseases are aggravated by malnutrition. There is no simple solution to urban malnutrition in a context plagued by underemployment and very low incomes.

The treatment of many of the health, educational, and habitat problems of large agglomerations will be made more difficult by the "semi-nomadism" of large groups in many developing countries. Seasonal and even weekly displacements from distant and even not so distant rural towns and areas to a region with main trading, industrial, and service centers is a common and quite possibly increasing trend for household heads (men or women) and for many single persons. It has become the major and often almost the only source of sufficient cash to purchase essential goods and often to feed a family. The living conditions of these masses of people are inevitably the worst to be found in any large agglomeration and very often involve entire families. No education system exists for these groups, and health services are for the most part those provided by the informal sector.

If the historic trends of the past two decades continue, then it is easy to predict that the new projects for conventional housing will be located in the same cities as at present, or in the same type of city, and will benefit the same income groups they favor now. In these circumstances, governments will concentrate their activities on acquiring land at the lowest possible price, improving the coordination of the agencies involved in funding, and reducing building and operating costs. If I am right, we shall be moving unwittingly towards metropolitan concentrations of 20, 25, or even 30 million inhabitants by clinging to past priorities, past planning approaches, norms that are irrelevant to the possibilities of the masses, and technologies that no government will be able to finance.

Most of the governments of the Third World countries were not elected by their subjects. The point of view of officialdom is therefore very different from that of the common citizen. The officials define the objectives of planning and programming from a perspective that has nothing in common with the population. Their points of view and their priorities are by nature different from the populations they control and are supposed to serve. Criteria vary with interest groups. If those who represent the administration were to enter into a dialogue with those for whom they are responsible, they would actually understand where their proposed "action-oriented planning" could lead. The mere existence of a plan does not necessarily make it a good plan. Most plans are not even legally approved. But how can the people discuss what is being done if they are not allowed to organize, and if they have no channels or mechanisms for entering into discussion with the administration?

The first step in developing a strategy is to examine its objective. If the objective of a settlement strategy is to benefit the lower classes and to satisfy their basic needs, the governments must drastically replan what they have been doing. It is quite clear that the housing situation for the great majority of the population is a consequence of their poverty, and unless the present levels of poverty are overcome, no solution exists. In other words, it is essential to attack the root causes that have led to the present situation in order to take action with any probability of success. The level of poverty is not the same in all countries, nor are the actual and potential means of livelihood comparable in each nation. But in all of them, it is necessary to create minimum conditions to make certain things happen, to achieve gradual progress. Yet what chances of success can be envisaged when the real purchasing power of the poor is declining and the cost of basic housing requirements goes up faster than any wage increase?

In addition, setting environmental norms, including those related to habitat (land use planning, housing, infrastructure and social buildings, etc.) is the responsibility of municipal government, but no municipal government in the Third World, including those of the capital cities, can cope with the financial and technical problems of building an adequate habitat for the masses of new dwellers. At the same time, securing adequate nutritional levels, controlling labor relations, establishing adequate environmental conditions in the work places and environmental standards for industrial plants, etc., and setting educational and sanitary standards, are the responsibility, in most countries, of national and/or state agencies. Central governments are assuming more and more control over all aspects of social and economic life with no apparent benefit to the lower income groups, at least in a majority of countries.

At the minimum, governments must offer their citizens coherent action—there must be a connection between what they promise and what they carry out. At the same time, they must solicit wide-ranging and unrestricted community participation that would allow them to learn from those who've built more than 50-60 percent of the underdeveloped cities, namely, the low-income population. In this way, the discussion about whether to favor big cities or the medium and small towns; whether to encourage investment in rural or in urban

areas; whether it is suitable to thin out the metropolitan areas or to build them up; whether this or that
technology is the more convenient or this or that priority is the more pressing will have a basis in reality.


## NOTES

[1]A summary of this analysis was recently published.
See Jorge E. Hardoy and David Satterthwaite, Shelter,
Need and Response (New York: John Wiley and Sons, 1981).
Teams from the Institute of Development Studies, Mysore
University; the Department of Architecture, University
of Khartoum; the Center for Urban and Regional Studies,
Buenos Aires; and the Faculty of Environmental Design,
Lagos University, participated in this project under the
coordination of the International Institute for Environment and Development. These teams have just embarked on
another study of the same subject, focused this time on
housing and human settlement policies in small economy
countries.
[2]Social statistics, especially those referring to
housing and settlements, are of poor quality in most developing countries. There are a number of reasons: (a)
until very recently, most governments paid scant
attention to the collection and presentation of vital
social statistics; (b) since most Third World governments are not interested in an explicit definition of
their position with regard to human settlements, such
statistics as are collected are fragmentary, scattered,
and more often than not irrelevant to the decisions that
need to be taken; (c) there is a lack of standardized
concepts and definitions; and (d) available information
does not have the required degree of area segregation to
make possible the formulation of more explicit social
policies.
[3]The seventeen countries studied by the four teams
were: India, the Philippines, Indonesia, Nepal, and
Singapore; Brazil, Bolivia, Colombia, and Mexico; Egypt,
Iraq, Sudan, Jordan, and Tunisia; Nigeria, Kenya, and
Tanzania. See R. P. Misra, ed., Habitat Asia, Issues
and Responses (New Delhi: Concept, 1979); Omer El Agraa
and Adil Ahmad, Assessment of Human Settlements in Arab
Countries (Khartoum: University of Khartoum Press,
1981); Beatriz Cuenya, Ruben Gazzoli, and Oscar
Yujnovsky, Políticas de asentamientos humanos, Cómision
Latinoamericana de Ciencias Sociales (CLACSO) (Buenos
Aires: SIAP, 1979); and David Aradeon et al., "Habitat
Evaluation in Sub-Saharan Africa" (in preparation).
[4]S.H.K. Yeh and A. Laquian, eds., Housing Asia's
Millions (Ottawa: International Development Research
Centre, 1979).

30

[5]"Given the new policies, programmes and government structures, the prospects for public housing in South East Asia are very bright." (Ibid. p. 29.)

[6]Two volumes were published by Ediciones SIAP, one dealing with the housing situation and the other with housing policies for low-income groups in the following cities: Mexico City, Mexico; Guatemala City, Guatemala; Bogotá, Colombia; Valencia, Venezuela; and Ciudad Guayana, Guayana; San Salvador, El Salvador; and Asunción, Paraguay. See Volume 1, La Vivienda a Bajo Costo, and Volume 2, Políticas del Estado en Materia de Vivienda, (Bogotá, Colombia: Sociedad Interamericana de Planificación, 1981).

[7]I should like to single out the Ph.D. thesis of A. Harth-Deneke, entitled "Towards Alternative Distributional Urban Strategies" (MIT, 1978), especially chapter 3, pp. 91-284. See also the case studies presented at the Seminar on Marginal Human Settlements, Jalapa, September 1977, collected by J. Bugnicourt and J. E. Hardoy in a special number of the Revista Interamericana de Planificación 14, no. 54 (June 1980).

[8]The twelve countries studied in this project under the coordination of the International Institute for Environment and Development were Bhutan, Fiji, and Papua-New Guinea; Somalia, Yemen, Arab Republic, and People's Democratic Republic of Yemen; Costa Rica, Panama, and Paraguay; and the Central African Republic, Sierra Leone, and Togo.

[9]Harry Richardson, "Population Redistribution Policies" (Paper delivered at the International Seminar on Small and Intermediate Centers, New Delhi, January 24-29, 1983.)

[10]P. L. Rosenfield, C. G. Widstrand, and A. P. Ruderman, "How Tropical Diseases Impede Social and Economic Development of Rural Communities: A Research Agenda," Rural Africana 8-9 (1980-1981):6

[11]In the small town of San Pedro (population: 30,000) in the province of Buenos Aires, Argentina, fourteen out of fifteen cases diagnosed with chagas disease were rural migrants attracted by the recently established industries.

[12]Ernest Feder, The Rape of Peasantry (New York: Doubleday and Co., 1971) p. 38.

[13]Here the text quotes the Brandt Report, North-South, a programme for survival (London: Pan Books, 1980), p. 106. It is interesting to note that the Brandt Report offers no suggestion at all on how to tackle this situation.

[14]The Hindustan Times (New Delhi), 24 January 1983, p. 5.

[15]Oscar Altimir, "La pobreza en America Latina," Revista de la CEPAL, no. 13 (April 1981):67-95. A recent report produced by PREALC for Latin America and the Caribbean states that in 1982 between 21.6 and 23

percent of the labor force was underused, a growth of
between 1.7 and 3.1 percent in relation to 1980, while
minimum (or basic) salaries, including industrial salaries, have deteriorated in these two years and are below
those in 1970 in real purchasing power. CEPAL, Notas de
la CEPAL, 372 (1982).

[16]Fundación Bariloche, "Catastrophe or New Society?
A Latin American World Model," IDRC; Ottawa, 1976; p.
65.

[17]Erik P. Eckholm, The Picture of Health (New York:
W. W. Norton and Company, 1977), passim.

[18]Few multilateral agencies commit more than 100
million U.S. dollars per year to shelter and related
projects. See Jorge E. Hardoy, "International Cooperation for Human Settlements," Latin American Research
Review 17, no. 3 (1982):3-28.

# Discussion

Okun: Your insistence upon active local participation is extremely important, but it raises a thorny issue. Virtually all the funds available for these projects--either from taxes, grants, or international loans--are funneled through central governments, and they make the decisions as to how the money is to be distributed. How do you expect us to change the locus of decisionmaking to the local level?

Crumley: Let me add another question to that one. Dr. Hardoy, you said that crowding was central to the main question with which we had to deal, and yet there are questions behind that that remain unanswered. Why are secondary centers neglected in favor of primary centers? What attempts have been made to understand the causes of increased migration into urban areas? We also have to discuss the problem of finding ourselves investigating phenomena about which we would hope to be neutral, at least initially, but which brings us in contact with circumstances central to revolution in the Third World. In other words, we find ourselves allied with Third World peoples, not their governments, and this may not be conducive to having those same Third World governments listen to our suggestions about change. So the manner in which we deal with this question, it seems to me, is extremely sensitive. What we have to do is present ourselves to the population in general and to those who run the government as cultural brokers, rather than as people who are particularly allied with one side or the other.

Hardoy: In the twenty traditional countries of Latin America, sixteen have a unitary system of government, and four have a federal system of government. Independent of the system of government, the trend to-

ward higher centralization in decisionmaking is obviously increasing. You find a federal system of government
in Mexico, where over 90 percent of public investment is
decided by the central government. The remaining investments go through municipal governments and provincial governments outside Mexico City. This phenomenal
concentration of resources in the central government has
been increasing over the last few years. However, among
the twenty traditional countries of Latin America, there
are a few that, although not truly representative of the
people themselves, do manage to maintain a certain
continuity in the election process. This means that the
key political parties (and I am referring here to Colombia, Costa Rica, and Venezuela) must attract voting of
some sort in order to continue their positions. Although it would be hard to prove, Dr. Crumley, I
think that you'll find in Colombia the greatest degree
of decentralization in the use of public resources of
any country in Latin America, with a very strong state
government, by comparison to other Latin American
countries. This strength is also true in Venezuela, although much less than in Colombia. The implication of
what I am saying is that reaching a certain type of representative government means a certain degree of decentralization in some aspects of the use of public funds
as well as in decisionmaking process.

Let me give you another example. During the period
of what you would call "progressive governments" in
Chile, the administrations of Eduardo Frei (1964-1970)
and Salvador Allende (1970-1973), there were some programs with enormous implications for the distribution
and welfare of the population. For instance, under the
agrarian reform program, people at the local and the
community levels, and at the level of the cooperative
farms and so on, were encouraged to participate and were
incorporated into the decisionmaking process. The urban migration trend decreased abruptly. Every human
being has a desire to participate in the decisions that
mold his or her life. In most of the Third World there
are very few truly representative governments. Most of
them are military governments; some are civilian governments, but supported by military elites. They have the
technocratic approach, the efficiency approach to everything they do, even if they are highly beneficent in
their actions. While this situation prevails, I see
very little chance of much improvement. We are increasingly moving into the newspapers and the mass media to
hit the elite where they hurt, and so on. But as researchers, we have a dual responsibility. One is to detect these things, and the other is not to neglect the
role of the people in all these processes; to do that we
must understand the people much better than we do. We
could be "co-guilty" in that in our research we also
follow the elitist approach, because of our training,

because of the way we think, and so on. We have a lot
to learn about how to improve the conditions of the
lower income groups by simply working with them and
letting them speak. If there is no other alternative,
then we can respond with books, in mass media, and so
on, about what these people think and believe. Because
the governments are truly insensitive we have to do more
than ever and really become advocates, what you would
call activists, using our knowledge, using our interpretation, if there are no other means of communication.

My hope is that there will be a trend toward the
reinforcement of local government at different levels.
There is a growing interest in the role of secondary
cities. But it will take time because the municipal
governments of these secondary cities have become the
middlemen between community groups and the central government. Someone has to negotiate this. The people
themselves can prevail. A beautiful example is that of
the shantytown, the so-called _barriadas_ or _pueblos
jovenes_ in Peru. It is the most researched problem in
shelter in all of Latin America. Since the fifties there
have been I don't know how many books, monographs, and
so on. It has attracted the attention of people from
many fields. The people of Peru have managed to form a
national association of shantytown dwellers. They have
proposed a law that has been sitting in congress for the
last eighteen months. Now you can go on researching the
problem of _barriadas_; you can go on putting socio-
logists, professionals, and student activists into the
field. You can probably continue motivating these
groups but you have to move a step forward. This is a
challenge to the national government by the people themselves, this national association of shantytown dwellers. Quite often, part of the role of the researcher
cum activist in the Third World is simply to provide the
means for an association like this to realize its
potential; to provoke the government. There is now a
law sitting there, and that law must be discussed, whether it passes or not. In other words, get these
groups that often fight for very specific gains--water
supply, transportation, and so on--into an organization
with a larger scope and greater political implications.

_Moser_: As an anthropologist who spent about ten
years working in low-income communities, mainly in Latin
America, I'm very interested in the discussion about the
nature of what goes on in low-income communities. This
is not something we can discuss in just one session, and
I hope it will carry right through the whole of the days
we're here. I would just like to make a couple of
points at this stage.

One is that in a sense I think it is helpful for us
to get away from both the attitude of the "conspiracy"
theory of government--and idea of corruption, neglect,
etc., on the part of government--and equally, the

perception that low-income settlements are hotbeds of revolution. I think we need a much clearer idea of the different interest groups that are involved in decision-making processes. What is very interesting if you look at the history of the attitude of government toward urban settlements is that you can see a very radical shift since the 1960s. Now, on the one hand, you could say that shift has occurred because the government felt threatened by low-income communities. In the 1960s, there was an attitude that a squatter settlement should be bulldozed. Now there has been a very clear shift (influenced by John Turner and others) toward letting lower-income people get on with it. An even further shift would be to say that actually we should help them a bit.

Now you may say that one of the political beliefs behind such a shift is that if we don't do it, the people will get up and revolt. The other way of looking at this is that there is also very clear recognition that the low-income population of the city is functional for the city's development; that it's providing a lot of cheap labor; that by assuming the costs of building homes, the population is actually lowering the amount of money the government has to put into resettlements. The interesting thing about such arguments is that they re-flect a shift and change on the part of interest groups within cities as to how they look at the needs of low income populations. So you get the mobilization approach to low income settlements.

That's one side of the story. The other side is that people actually are getting on with building their own homes; people are getting on with mobilizing. The critical element is the extent to which low-income communities perceive the problems of their housing as problems, not individual problems, but community prob-lems. When you get to that situation, you get the beginnings of people who will mobilize, who will iden-tify those who have the power to allocate resources, and go to work with them. Of course you get political par-ties coming in, you get interest groups coming in, you get anthropologists coming in, and so on--but let's not forget that there are people who live there, who stay there, and who actually do get on with organizing them-selves. Their capacity to organize, apart from outside constraints, is very much influenced by the extent to which they see their problem as a collective problem.

In Latin American cities, people do not assume that housing is an individual issue. They assume it is an issue that involves the community. They may cope with it as individuals, depending on their income level and function, but they may also organize, mobilize, invade land, take over territory, etc. An interesting link be-tween housing and health is the current extent to which health needs also are perceived by low-income communities as an issue involving the collective, rather than a problem of bad parenting or lack of individual income to get water in a household.

Donahue: My work at UNICEF is almost always a practical, down-to-earth, "let's see what we can do today" approach to helping governments solve the problems of women and children in poor urban areas. It's not academic, it's not intellectual, and in many ways, it doesn't fit within the context of what we might call "good, sound urban and regional planning." You might consider it sort of a fire brigade, putting fires out right now and seeing what we learn from that. So my perspective reflects that kind of experience, gained especially over the last five years. Our organization has gone from three or four programs to almost fifty--in Latin America, Asia, and, soon, Africa.

Two years ago when we were preparing a major policy review of our support to urban programs in developing countries, we asked the population division of the U.N. to do some special runs of their latest demographic information, coming out of the late 1970s census information. What we found when we asked them to look at what I label "the absorption rate" was, even for me, shocking. Now two-thirds of all growth in developing countries takes place in cities. By the end of this century, over 80 percent of all population increase in developing countries will be taking place in cities. There is at least one U.N. demographic region, made up of a number of countries in Asia, where urban growth exceeds total population growth of the countries in that region. China's urban growth rate is greater than 50 percent. I think one of the forecasts says that within the next twenty years, the Chinese urban growth rate will be over 100 percent, an urban growth rate greater than the total country increase. That, at a time when fertility levels look like they will level off. This curve can't go on indefinitely.

Another piece of research came up with the fact that natural increase is now responsible for an average of 61 percent of urban population growth in developing countries, compared with only 39 percent from rural migration. It's a document called "Patterns of Urban and Rural Population Growth" put out by the U.N. about two years ago. It seems to me that it introduces a factor that not many people are looking at very carefully in the context of urban trends, urbanization, policy planning, and the whole gamut of things that we consider our bailiwick. The fact is that migration is not as significant now as a lot of people think it is. When you read statements that say (I read this a few weeks ago) "45 percent of all growth in Lima is based on migration," you know the converse is also true--55 percent is from natural increase. If you built a wall around Mexico City right now, there would probably be 25

instead of 32 million people at the end of the century,
and what is the real difference between the two? I think
for those of us concerned with these issues, and especially concerned with dealing in a practical way, ad-
vocating policy changes, focusing on critical factors,
we have to come to grips with what in the U.N. is
euphemistically called "responsible parenting." If
you're looking at urbanization, this is a really
critical and difficult issue and fundamentally important
in terms of the resolution of the things we're talking
about here.

UNICEF established a policy framework five or six
years ago that is basically a participatory course in
development. Start with people where they are and work
with them. Seek out ways to build bridges between
government agencies and people. Focus on low-cost,
cost-effective actions. Members of the community have
to be involved in the selection of people that are
supposed to be the first in line of service. If it's
primary health care, the health-care worker must reflect
some real choice on the part of the people in the
community. When there is no community involvement in
the selection,things don't work very well. We find that
participation gets defined quite differently from place
to place. Yet one very powerful lesson that we've
learned is, "Don't presume people aren't organized."
This is a critical message one gets from the research in
Latin America. Even in our work in Lima that started
five years ago, and what has probably been one of the
more effective urban primary health - care programs
functioning now in developing countries, with lots of
problems, the work began with an organized community of
500,000 people in the southern part of Lima. It was a
barriada that was settled by trade unionists who were
powerful, organized, knew how to do analysis as well as
professionals, and knew how to protect their interests.
So there was a framework you could work in, that you
could build on. We sat outside of Arequipa, where the
program is being expanded by the government; we sat with
the mayor of one of the outlying cities that is
basically a big barriada, a big low-income area, with
the president of the association of low-income areas of
Arequipa, sat and negotiated, discussed where we'd be
going over the next few years. . . .

It seems difficult. There are indications that this
is feasible, but it takes time. It can be painful. You
can't control all the resources. We've learned over the
past five years to be realistic in our expectations. We
have found in enough places now that you can focus on
relatively small-scale demonstration programs and le-
verage them. From a program started with 50,000 people
in India, we are now supporting two national programs,
one focused on urban community development in the big
cities, one on urban community development in the small

to middle-sized towns, and they're two major national policies. They are policies of the government.

This experience raises very serious questions in my own mind about a field that I'm trained in and have worked in--the relevance of urban planning to the kinds of things that we're doing, and the relevance of focusing on housing as an issue. There's a question in my mind whether housing is the critical issue. There are other things that are more critical. I think in many of the cities UNICEF works in, when you look at the urban planning function, you find that, unlike practice in Europe and North America, either urban planners have a much more powerful political role than you might expect from the way planning is technically addressed in North America and Europe, and they're dealing in the political realm through the mechanism of planning, or in fact they're really on the margin of things and have very little to do with the forces that cause and affect the issues that Jorge discussed this morning.

Hardoy: I would like to pose a question for the health professionals among us. The basic issues of social welfare have prompted many community groups to organize in an effort to improve their lot. Is the same true with reference to health issues? Have people tried to organize in order to improve their standards of health? Unions, churches, and other groups make jobs and, on occasion, shelter, issues of major concern. Professionals such as architects and engineers often make public statements and try to influence politicians on the shelter issue. But I know of no instance in which this has been done for health issues. Is this because I am not familiar enough with the health issues, or because those issues have not attracted the same public attention as have shelter issues?

Miller: It seems to me that it is the nature of public health to be a highly centralized activity with priorities that tend to be set by central authorities. There are analysts and observers who have said that it's very difficult to identify any kind of public health measure of consequence that has not resulted, to one degree or another, in the loss of some individual and even local initiatives and freedoms. Decisions such as how one will dispose of waste water require a degree of organization that tends to limit local action. But it seems to me that there is some evidence that even though the priorities and the finances may be determined centrally, implementation is really a local phenomenon. Specifically, there are instances in which populations have exercised their own initiatives to achieve improved health; they are rare, but they do exist. Populations have done that in relation to pestilence and epidemic disease, in relation to nutritional problems, in their concern and anger over food access and distribution. I'm not sure that they've done it around habitation and shelter, but it seems to me that around survival issues, populations have if not exercised their own initiatives, at least demanded that initiative be taken on their behalf.

In all this I think it's terribly important to emphasize, as you have done, the multiple determinants of health and separate them a little, or at least define them a little, away from medical care. I don't know of populations that have exercised strong demand for extension of access to medical care, except as that's been promoted by public groups, but I can think of populations that have exercised initiatives to relieve themselves of the economic burden of achieving access to medical care. I don't think that it's really possible to promote health necessities for a population as a bootstrap, do-it-yourself movement. I think it requires a degree of priority setting, organization, and central financing, though I think these are feasible only if there are mechanisms by which local groups can determine what the processes and interventions are that are most appropriate.

Tulchin: There are examples with which I'm familiar of groups organizing around, certainly, water issues, which are as directly related to health as they are to habitat, and so it's questionable whether we can make the kind of distinction that you suggest. In one case with which I am familiar, in Bahia, Brazil, in 1970, two-thirds of the adult residents of the favela registered for the mayoral elections on a single-issue platform of water. For the first time in history, each mayoral candidate gave election speeches promising them water.

Then in recent negotiations between a major national Mexican union group with the Secretary of Labor, the union demanded a 60 percent wage increase to catch up to inflation. The government, as part of a deal with the International Monetary Fund, had promised not to allow a wage increase that high. The wage increase was set at 20-25 percent, but the government conceded to the union an increase in the number of union hospitals and pharmacies. This, perhaps, proves your point indirectly that it is a fall-back issue, but there are examples of the health issue being part of interest group articulation or a source of stimulus for organizing the community.

It seems to me that there's a challenge embedded in your argument. You suggest that the efficiency paradigm in the study of development is deficient, and you criticized it in a number of ways. As students of the development process, it's hard to find an alternate paradigm if the efficient allocation of resources is not the best way to proceed in Third World countries to generate ever higher levels of goods and services across the society. What other method do you have in mind?

That on the analytical level. On the level of development assistance, where many of us have attempted to work, given the nature of financing, one runs smack up against the issue of centralization and Dan Okun's question about where our interventions will be. With which international, bi-national, or national organization will we operate? In general, projects to improve health delivery, water supply, or housing are a reaction, either positive or negative, to national priorities set by those very governments whom you have determined are essentially unrepresentative and, perhaps, ineffective and inefficient in the allocation of resources. So there is a real pragmatic issue that requires our attention. How do you penetrate the system? Where do you go? Even John Donahue's description of working at the margin with small groups inevitably involves dealing with government entities, official groups, and national groups. So there's both an analytical and a strategic problem that you pose, and they seem to intersect. I'm a little uncertain as to how we can separate them to deal with them, or if they can be separated.

Hardoy: Let's return to John Turner's studies in Lima. After working for several years in the pueblo, he came up with a set of five priorities as defined by the government in relation to housing policies for the big cities of Peru, and especially for Lima--one, two, three, four, five. Then he put those questions to the pueblo dwellers and asked them to put the questions in order of priority, and the order of priority was five, four, three, two, one. The same five things, as seen by the pueblo dwellers, were exactly the opposite of what the government was attempting to do. So the problem is not whether the development agencies in one government or organization are efficient or not; it is who decides on the priority, and for whom is this development oriented? The two completely different worlds have two different sets of priorities. If you talk to people living today (June 1983) in Argentina, the number one priority for them is simply to have access to a minimum income that will permit them to eat. The government would never list that as a priority. If we truly are interested in development, then we must find out, as researchers, what are the true needs of the people.

Tulchin: I want to comment on the notion of a society making a decision to provide on a universal basis certain minimum levels of services, whatever that package of services might be. That called to mind our previous discussion of priorities. What are our priorities in training health professionals, whether they be paramedics, doctors, or something else? Recently, two of our medical students returned to Chapel Hill from a very informal internship in Nicaragua. They described an experience that to the best of my knowledge is not fully articulated in national policy, but it is pertinent to our conversation.

First of all, there has been a priority change in Nicaragua since 1979. At the governmental level, the decision to provide on a universal basis certain minimum services has been articulated. Those include things with which we're all familiar: packets for infant oral rehydration, inoculation against certain common infant diseases, what we might call a patient-care program, and water provision. These four are within a broad medical care plan. What's happened is that they've set up district health centers across the country, including small and intermediate settlements as well as rural areas. They've distributed to these facilities the most sophisticatedly trained personnel as they have. The fourth year medical student from UNC was one of the best people they had in her center. She was the head of a team of nurse practitioners. These people would set up like the old Indian market. Within six months of this program, the percentage of the population of Nicaragua that had contact on a periodic basis with a health care worker-- frequency was about once a month--increased from something like 20-25 percent on a national basis to somewhere between 75 and 80 percent, and it's rising.

So, clearly, the question of social priorities is critical to an understanding of these issues. It's not merely a matter of who's the most effective medic in a particular area or what level of training should be sought, nor even what the cost is. The second issue, universality at a societal level or the absence of it, is a central issue that runs through all of the cases that we've been describing. The Cuban case is a very different plan of health delivery from the Nicaraguan one, the examples in Yugoslavia that were discussed, and so on. When you start to change the society's priorities, the measurement of how much a particular medical service or health service costs changes. The effectiveness of a particular service must vary--whether or not COPC is a high-cost demonstration effect, or whether it's the only thing you can do under certain social organizations will be the question.

Bear in mind that our geographic focus is the Third World. It's hard to export certain notions of the distribution of medical personnel in a market economy, particularly a market economy such as ours that is unusually well-endowed. You can go to other market economies in the western world where the level of resource endowment is not so great, and you find alternate modes of distribution, as in Sweden or other western European countries. So it is even more difficult to project this kind of training into the Third World.

Miller: Again, regarding the issue of costs, you're quite right--the costs of the community-oriented primary care are not greater; if anything, they're less

than the fragmented service programs for comparable
census banks. But still, the cost, I think, is beyond
what we ordinarily conceive of as reasonable to pay for
a package of services that we'd made universally available to the population. In terms of social priorities,
I just want to point out that those wonderful WHO oral
rehydration packets will soon be distributed under the
supervision of a physician only!

Tulchin: I'd like to return to my description of
the Nicaraguan situation. I described the experience of
only one of the medical students. The other was on duty
at the intensive-care unit in the largest, most
sophisticated hospital in Managua. Their experiences
were at opposite poles. You can't get more tertiary, in
Nicaragua, than the experience of this second student.
He said, essentially, that the hospital was under-
utilized because of the gap between primary and tertiary
care. It had become an evolving discussion in the
Ministry of Health, to make conscious and explicit the
results of their serendipitous experience in these primary health centers.

Madison: In Cuba, in the years following the
revolution, they had very few doctors, and they were
facing serious nationwide health problems, not new
problems, but ones they'd always faced. They did very
much the same thing as the students described as happening in Nicaragua. The Cubans took these actions
across the country, according to what the priorities
were. That is, people were trained who lived in a kind
of infrastructure of community participation, and only
as they trained sufficient doctors did they begin to put
doctors in there and make those public health programs
into polyclinics. And then only as they got the basic
level of medical care services around the polyclinics
did they go to--and they're still doing this--the
concept of community-oriented primary care. This simply
means that the local care does more than the nationally
mandated services and the basic pain and suffering
stuff. The people begin to investigate their own community, to determine its local needs, and reformulate
programs according to what they find there. So it seems
to me that all these are stages in an evolutionary
process. Maybe the last stage is a fully developed
community-oriented primary care program where every
community has its own health program that is responsive
partly to national priorities. But in large part the
program is whatever the community determines it needs
most.

# CHAPTER 2

# Preventive Planning: What Are We Planning to Prevent?

## DAVID SATTERTHWAITE

The title "preventive planning" is somewhat ambiguous. It does not make clear what planning is trying to prevent. The issue under consideration here is whether settlement planning can (or does) prevent or lessen problems inherent in the search of lower income groups for adequate accommodation and a healthy living environment.

Since "settlement planning" can cover a very wide range of measures that impinge on health--including transport planning and planning to promote regional economic development--this chapter considers only three aspects of planning as they relate to housing and basic services. The first can be termed "negative controls," i.e., the official regulations, norms, codes, and standards that seek to regulate the private sector's use of land and construction activities. The second can be termed "positive initiatives" and includes government-initiated new developments. The third concerns the policies that govern the installation of infrastructure and services.

This focus excludes some essential issues in planning and healthy housing. One is the extent to which the whole scope of settlement planning is defined and conditioned by legislation and by the concepts of individual property rights in force in each nation. The evolution of the land tenure system and the legislative base of each nation must be understood if settlement planning's present role in ameliorating the housing-health problems of the poor is to be defined. The differences between nations and regions will not be investigated here since the focus of this discussion is

44

the Third World as a whole.  In order to set a context
for preventive planning, however, a brief historical introduction to government involvement in city planning
and health care delivery follows.


BACKGROUND

Planning often plays an antagonistic role to the search
by income groups for adequate, healthy accommodation.
Much of the early impetus behind government intervention
in the development of cities in Europe and North America
was to protect the health and environment of upper
income groups and to prevent their "contamination" by
the poorer masses.
    The need for strong public intervention in city de-
velopment arose from the chaos generated by cities that
grew rapidly and without controls during the nineteenth
and early twentieth centuries.  Prior to this, the vast
majority of the population lived outside cities.  Only
when urban areas (and especially larger cities) became
the main centers of production and population, and when
rapid urban growth became common, did public controls
and public institutions to enforce them become standard
practice.  Legislation concerning public health, the
health problems of working-class housing, and initiatives to open up, widen, or straighten streets predate
the idea of city planning as a normal function of government by many decades.  Over time, in a rather ad hoc
manner, a whole battery of public controls evolved that
dealt with, for instance, construction activities or the
use to which land could be put.  The first systematic
attempts to control housing quality (i.e., to guarantee
some minimum standards) date from the mid-nineteenth
century, as do the beginnings of large "social housing
programs."[1]  It is hardly surprising that such initiatives arose.  The life expectancy of the laboring class
in cities like Manchester and Liverpool in the early
nineteenth century was between fifteen and seventeen
years. The upper classes' life expectancy was more than
double this.[2]
    Although social reformers had been fighting for the
improvement of housing conditions for lower income
groups, it was the more tangible threat of cholera that
gave impetus to the most basic forms of preventive
planning--piped water, hygienic disposal of human
wastes, garbage collection, street cleaning, and some
controls on standards in rental accommodation. Cholera,
unlike many diseases prevalent among lower income
groups, affected rich and poor alike. Furthermore,
cholera epidemics were very bad for business and those
who could afford to do so usually fled the city when
there was the threat of an epidemic.  It took two major
cholera epidemics in London in 1831-1832 and 1848-1849

to make government recognize its responsibility in ensuring a safer supply of piped water and the construction of a sewer system. In New York, there were similar
problems of inertia, despite cholera epidemics in 1832
and 1849. Although the first signs of some city government concern in health issues were somewhat earlier,
it wasn't until 1866 that New York had a Metropolitan
Board of Health with the power to undertake preventive
measures against cholera. New York's success in warding
off the 1866 epidemic greatly encouraged other cities to
follow its example.[3]

But more effective preventive planning in Western
nations, in the form of measures to prevent the health
problems inherent in uncontrolled city growth and
building construction, took far longer. The diseases of
poverty, such as malnutrition, typhoid, and tuberculosis, flourished. Little was done to combat them
since they impinged far less on the health of wealthier
citizens. When, in England, trends in adult mortality
changed, beginning in the 1870s, it was due more to
clean water, better sanitation, increased purchasing
power among lower income groups, and cheaper foodstuffs
and soap than to any improvement in housing conditions.
A report in 1907 quoting census data, said that 38,000
Londoners lived six or more to a room. The report also
noted that the death rate in different districts rose in
proportion to the increase in single-room tenement dwellings and the number of families living in them.[4]

Meanwhile, in the Asian and African "colonies," a
rather more radical form of preventive planning developed: the strict spatial segregation of whites from
"coloreds" and "natives." Health concerns were a major
factor in initiating segregation although questions of
social control were also important. For instance, in
Nigeria, European and non-European residential areas
were separated by a building-free zone 440 yards wide
that was considered farther than a malarial mosquito
could travel.[5] In Morocco, the new cities for European
settlers were built at some distance from the old cities
of Fez and Marrakesh and were separated by a cordon
sanitaire.[6] The often-used term for the exclusively
white residential areas in colonial cities was "the sanitary district," and this was not a misnomer. Within
these white enclaves, high infrastructure and service
standards were met. Piped water was provided; so too
were sewers. Densities were very low. In Delhi in 1931,
there were 50,000 "natives" per square mile in the old
city and its suburbs. In New Delhi, the capital built
by the British for the British, there were less than
2000 people per square mile. In May 1929, infant
mortality in the old walled city was 512 per 1000, while
in New Delhi, it was 82 per 1000 in 1932. Death rates
in the old city were between 30 and 47 per 1000; they
were 9 per 1000 in New Delhi.[7]

In addition, hospitals and health services were set up essentially to serve the needs of the colonial elite. The high concentration today of doctors and medical facilities in the main city of many African and Asian nations has its origin in the health services set up in colonial times. Medical research during colonial rule was geared more to the diseases that threatened the white elite (such as malaria and sleeping sickness) than it was to the most widespread, dangerous, and debilitating diseases that affected the native population.[8]

Perhaps the most fundamental colonial legacy to planning was the introduction or strengthening of land tenure systems that gave the individual a right to own or use land. Europeans grabbed desirable land, and they used laws and concepts of land tenure to sanction this that were alien to the indigenous population. These laws and concepts protected the rights of those who owned or had freehold tenure to land against those with none. They continue to do so today. As more people and the land they lived on were drawn into a cash economy, access to land become increasingly determined by ability to pay for it. One of the most fundamental problems confronting planners in the Third World today--the fact that many city inhabitants cannot get housing plots with secure legal tenure--can be traced back to this legacy. While the inhabitants of the illegal shantytowns provide the city with cheap labor and cheap goods and services, the land tenure system does not provide for their housing needs.

The legislative legacy of colonialism is easily seen in building codes and standards designed originally to provide Europeans with high housing and health standards. A report in 1978 noted that most of the formal standards and criteria applied to shelter provision in Africa, Asia, and Latin America even today are clearly recognizable extensions of similar normative requirements in Britain, France, Spain, and Portugal in the nineteenth and early twentieth centuries.[9] Thus, the emphasis they often give to imported building materials and to certain design features was put there to ensure that colonial officials and other Europeans received something not too dissimilar to the standards they expected in their home country.

In Latin America, the situation is somewhat different; nations had achieved independence early in the nineteenth century when cities were small and not growing rapidly. As in Europe and North America, concern with preventive planning really began after the major epidemics had greatly increased death rates. In this instance, standards were borrowed from Europe and North America. The early concentration in the major cities was on the installation of piped water, garbage collection in central districts, the opening up or widening and paving of streets, and, although somewhat later, the construction of sewerage systems.

Urban physical planning techniques in the Third World also followed western models. Only in this century did public authorities in the West begin in a positive way to try and guide the growth and development of expanding cities. The "City Beautiful" and the "Garden City" movements gave impetus to this. Few questioned the transfer of techniques and experiences from the West to the Third World, despite the phenomenal differences in local conditions and in the institutional structures that were meant to implement the plans. After all, most new city plans were prepared by western planners or by those trained in western planning schools. Even with the development of planning schools in the Third World, the curricula remained firmly based on western models, and in many African and Asian nations, the colonial legacy of laws, regulations, and institutions remained very strong. In British colonies in Africa, with the enactment of comprehensive Town and Country Planning laws in the United Kingdom, colonial administrators began to adopt the English planning system with its structure and procedure.[10] While inappropriate planning techniques still in force today cannot be blamed entirely on the colonial past, these are embedded in the entire legislative structures of these nations and are difficult to change.[11] The revision of these planning systems often demands more fundamental revisions to legislation. As Kanyeihamba pointed out, for Anglophonic Africa, planners' powers are contained in statutes, rules, regulations, and judicial precedents drafted and created by members of the legal profession.[12] Lawyers tend to be protective of the rights of property owners. This hardly meshes with planners' roles in guaranteeing lower income groups access to secure land plots.

At first, the largely static master plan, another European legacy, with its accompanying controls over land use, became the most common form of city planning in the Third World, despite the fact that most master plans remained largely unimplemented. Many of their components were unimplementable. The institutional structure, trained manpower, funds, or political will—or all four--did not exist to implement them. A recent World Bank paper noted that "land use regulation is almost a complete failure as a policy intended to implement a land use plan to meet current needs for land by all income groups at a reasonable price, to permit orderly changes, and to increase property tax revenue."[13] More flexible city planning techniques or city-region planning measures have increasingly replaced the static master plan. But even with these, the unwillingness (or inability) of governments to tackle the roots of uncontrolled city growth also has led to lack of implementation or impact.

Another response to the failure of city planning
was a concentration on certain projects, such as slum or
squatter upgrading projects or serviced site schemes.
These, being far smaller and more focused in scale,
generally met with more success in what was defined
earlier as "preventive planning"--planning measures that
prevent or lessen problems inherent in lower income
groups' search for adequate accommodation and a healthy
living environment. However, most of these projects are
small, and they reach only a small proportion of those
in need. The lessons of the more successful schemes--
that the most effective planning approach is to ignore
existing building codes and standards, concentrate on
basic levels of service for all, involve the people
themselves in plan preparation and implementation--are
not applied or accepted in citywide or nationwide
programs.

**PREVENTING WHAT?**

Thus, today, "planning" in the context of city planning
is achieving little addressing poorer citizens' housing
and health needs. Yet planning in theory has some role
to play, even though the problems of health and of
disease control, like the problem of poverty, are rooted
in social, economic, and political factors that planning
cannot change. As Hardoy states in the opening chapter
of this volume, the very idea of public intervention in
housing should be to ensure that a group of people
obtains some mix of the following elements: more secure
tenure, better protection from natural elements (weather, floods, earthquakes, etc.), more room, access to
safe drinking water, more hygienic and more convenient
disposal of household and human wastes, access to cheap
building materials, and access to job or income opportunities. Some mix of these elements should be provided at a price that lower income groups can afford and
that does not involve a high unit subsidy that would
limit the number of people the initiative could reach.
Clearly, planning should and could play a considerable
role in this, especially in making available appropriate
sites for low-income housing, where the needs of lower
income groups for tenure, locations, affordable cost,
site safety, and infrastructure and services could be
met.

But today, the whole battery of norms, codes, and
regulations that are meant to guide and control housing
construction and city growth are ignored by most new
housing developments. They are ignored because they
demand a form and type of house, certain fittings and
fixtures, housing layout, and settlement pattern that
are far beyond the resources of lower income groups. It
is worth recalling that in most large Third World

cities, a third or more of the population live on illegally occupied or subdivided land.[14] They do not live on legal house plots that are part of some city plan because such plots are far too expensive. They do not live in houses constructed to official building codes or standards because, again, such housing is too expensive for them. They usually do not receive basic services like piped water, sewers, public transport, garbage removal, and so on, because their houses are "illegal" and outside the city plan. The building and planning standards enshrined as official norms or in official codes guarantee that the poor majority can never afford an official, legal house.

Perhaps the three most serious ways in which planning controls inhibit low-cost housing construction are in land use controls, building regulations, and procedures for obtaining official support for house construction or improvement. Land use controls, such as minimum building plot sizes or zoning defining densities, do not allow small plots. So plot prices are kept high. While officially acceptable plot sizes may be 200 square meters, the average in illegal shantytowns is often below 20 square meters. Large minimum plot sizes have the "advantage" of keeping land prices too high in the wealthier residential districts for the "poor" to be able to afford them. This does little to aid the revision of existing regulations.

Building codes and regulations often demand that houses be built to unrealistic specifications or use materials that are no longer available or are unnecessarily expensive. Many codes demand the use of imported materials and expressly forbid the use of widely available local materials. Or they demand minimum ceiling heights or room sizes unrelated to health or safety needs. The codes and regulations tend to be complex and full of technical terms. Madras City Corporation's Building Rules, which apply to all buildings within the city, are couched in legal language and technical terms far beyond the understanding of most lay builders. For instance, "the level of foundation shall be such that the minimum depth of the foundation to prevent the soil moving laterally under pressure shall be according to Rankine's theory." Rankine's theory is then set out in mathematical symbols with no diagrams, drawings, or simple explanations of what is required.[15] Finally, the procedure demanded for obtaining official permission to build, improve, or extend a house is often complicated and expensive. In Papua-New Guinea, one cannot legally build a house which contravenes the Land Act, the Health Act, or the Town Planning Act. In practice this means that a builder must get the signatures of six bureaucrats in different offices scattered throughout the capital, and then he still must wait until he receives the endorsement of the Building Board.[16]

## NEGATIVE CONTROLS

In looking at preventive planning, one can divide
planning measures into negative controls (i.e., restrictions on private sector activities), positive measures,
and public investments in infrastructure and services.
The purpose of negative controls--in theory--is to
promote better quality living environments and to ensure
that a basic level of health and safety standards is
attained in housing and in settlements. As we noted
earlier, negative controls tend to play the opposite
role by setting standards that the poor majority cannot
meet. Negative controls can only promote health and
safety if they strike a balance between what is desirable (in terms of health and safety), attainable (by all
levels of construction operation), and affordable (by
the majority of households). Otherwise they will continue to be irrelevant to the housing and health needs
of lower income groups.

With regard to housing standards, it is obvious
that attaining even minimum standards in terms of
density of occupation, structural stability, illumina-
tion, and so on may be impossible for a large sector of
the population. The basic problem faced by low-income
groups remains the same as it was for the working
classes who poured into European and North American
cities in the nineteenth and early twentieth centuries--
they lack the income to afford sufficient food, let
alone pay for an adequate house or room. This problem
will never be solved by any housing or planning
strategy. It depends far more on adequate incomes and
adequate diets.[17] However, revised negative controls
can lower greatly the cost of a legal housing unit.
Thus, they can remove the illegal status that characterizes so many low-income housing developments in Third
World cities. And, in so doing, undermine the reasons
given by municipal authorities for not providing basic
services and infrastructure.

In some instances, perhaps, no building standards
should be demanded. Khartoum in the Sudan, for example,
evolved an interesting standards policy in this regard.
Residential areas are divided into first, second, third,
and fourth class areas. In fourth class areas, no
building standards are demanded. Lowest income groups
can live there and build legally, whatever they construct. But infrastructure and service provision to
fourth class areas is minimal, and leases for house
sites are relatively short. In third class areas,
certain minimum standards are demanded, and here infrastructure and service provision standards are higher,
lot sizes are larger, and leases are longer. There is a
progression in standards in terms of infrastructure and

services, lot size, and lease length up to second and
first class areas. Housing areas can be upgraded from,
say, third to second class. The city is not divided
into large first class and second class areas well away
from third and fourth class areas. Different class areas
are usually mixed together. While there are problems
actually implementing this policy, and there is a huge
backlog in service provision, the principle of flexible
and upgradable standards remains sound. There must be
provision for those who can afford to spend little or
nothing on housing.

Reducing standards and controls to mesh best with
local social, economic, and health conditions can lower
the cost of a legal house. But perhaps a more important
step is to change the whole emphasis of negative
controls away from "negative." If the purpose of negative controls is to promote health and safety, then
these should not be negative controls but active promotion of basic improvements. If largely self-built and
self-managed illegal neighborhoods are responsible for
much of the new housing construction within a city--and
this is usually the case in Third World cities--then the
approach has to change completely if the promotion of
health and safety is the aim. In these illegal settlements, the people are solving their own housing problems with no public help. They often do so in the face
of strong opposition from government. The houses and
settlements so built, despite the lack of services and
the often poor quality of the houses, actually meet
their inhabitants' housing needs in terms of cost, location, access to family and friends, access to income
sources, and capacity for home expansion and/or extension. Official housing or serviced-site scheme
housing would be far less effective in the same circumstances.

Once city authorities finally acknowledge that
there is no alternative to these "illegal" settlements,
what is the role of the planner? In existing settlements, preventive planning has to include planning measures that tackle health and safety questions and are
seen by the people as effective and affordable. Thus,
instead of seeking to enforce negative controls for
those who cannot afford to meet them, a planning program
could offer advice on how to meet health and safety
standards at minimum cost. City planning offices could
be supplemented by building advice centers, decentralized to the neighborhood level where self-built settlements are developing.

But for such building advice centers to be effective, there has to be a clear understanding of the
connections between housing and health. At the level of
the house itself, there must be an understanding of how
to articulate standards that reduce health problems at
the lowest possible cost. For instance, advisory pos-

ters and pamphlets produced in conjunction with neighborhood people could address the relaionship between tuberculosis and poor ventilation plus overcrowding and suggest ways to lessen such health risks. An effort such as this is likely to be far more effective than an attempt to impose certain technical standards. But this implies an intimate knowledge of the health and disease control problems in each settlement and a continuing dialogue with the inhabitants of that settlement. Both are very rare in city governments. Pioneering work has been done by informally organized groups within low income settlements at their own initiative and by nongovernment organizations such as church groups or charities working with low-income settlement inhabitants. But official recognition for such approaches is very rare.

## POSITIVE ACTION

The major preventive planning role of governments is to attack those constraints at city and national levels that push up the cost and limit the supply of housing components: house sites, finance for the construction or improvement of dwellings, public provision of water, disposal of household and human wastes, public roads and footpaths, electricity, and such services as primary health care, education, and public transport.

In larger and more rapidly growing cities, the provision of legal and affordable house plots as alternatives to squatting or illegal subdivisions is fundamental. At present, the growth of cities is uncontrolled because most new housing has to be built illegally. Without appropriate public intervention to lower the cost and greatly increase the supply of legal, serviced housing plots to match the needs of lower income groups --in terms of cost and access to income sources as much as in terms of basic service provision--no sustained improvement in housing conditions is possible.

If public authorities boost the supply of serviced housing plots within the context of a coherent city plan, this could bring with it many advantages in terms of preventive planning. First, it could provide lower income groups with healthier and less dangerous alternatives to the sites they are often forced onto--slopes subject to landslides, floodplains, swamps, or tidal basins. Second, installing infrastructure and services in new sites prior to house construction could mean far lower unit costs than installing infrastructure and services in response to the unplanned growth of residential areas in and around the city. Illegal settlements spring up all over the city wherever the inhabitants feel they have some chance of avoiding forcible eviction. This produces an unplanned mosaic of high- and low-density

occupation that enormously increases the cost of installing roads, electricity, sewers, piped water, and so
on. Third, if such an initiative were done on a considerable scale, it could act as a downward pressure on
residential land prices throughout the city. Of course,
a significant constraint remains: well-located land has
a market value that pushes it beyond the prices lower
income groups can afford. Yet the poorer households
very often need a more central location that minimizes
travel and time costs incurred in getting to a job or
source of income. Governments rarely have sufficient
commitment to the needs of the poor to expropriate well-
located urban land at prices that allow its allocation
for low-income housing developments.

The various means by which public agencies can
guide and control the urban land market cannot be summarized here. Each nation or region will have tradi-
tions of land tenure and transfer and existing legislation that will condition the form public initiatives
have to take. But the goal remains the same--the
provision of legal alternatives to squatting that match
lower income groups' needs and resources. This implies
changes in legislation for public expropriation of land
"in the public interest," with precisely defined criteria for establishing compensation. It implies tough
penalties for landowners who leave urban land holdings
undeveloped because of the speculative gains this
brings. It implies city governments with trained manpower and resources able to enforce such a policy and
develop a fiscal base that allows for long-term investment programs in infrastructure and services.

But the reality in most Third World nations is in
stark contrast to this. Most governments in theory have
the power to expropriate land "in the public interest,"
but few are prepared to do so to ease the housing problems of lower income groups. City governments remain
weak. With the centralization of power and resources,
national agencies often have taken over city-level
functions such as infrastructure construction. National
governments frequently have appropriated local taxes and
replaced them with inadequate grants to local authorities. The actual grants given by national governments
to city authorities are often the first to be cut when
funds are needed for other purposes. Under such
conditions, there is little chance that city governments
will be able to plan investments in infrastructure and
services. In addition, most city governments do not
have up-to-date cadastral surveys that define who owns
(or has the right to) what land. Many city governments
do not even have an up-to-date map of the city itself.
Yet these are the most fundamental preconditions for
more control over the land market and a stronger fiscal
base from land taxes.

The experience of Tunisia over the last decade provides an interesting example of a national government struggling to come to terms with these kinds of issues. In the early seventies, a political commitment was made to improve housing conditions of lower income groups. The public housing program was greatly expanded. Central government cancelled municipal debts, and efforts were made to strengthen local government planning capacities and funding base. A new land agency for residential developments was set up to acquire land in or close to urban areas in advance of need, install infrastructure and services, and then sell it. In so doing, it increased the supply of land developed for housing and allowed new residential developments to conform to city plans. A rolling program of land acquisition, development, and sale avoided the expense of tying up capital in a "land bank." The public housing agency also had powers to expropriate the land needed for the housing program and had access to state land to keep unit costs down. But despite this massive program relative to population size, insufficient units were built. Despite substantial subsidies for public housing units, the lowest income groups could still not afford them, and often public housing units did not match the needs of lower income groups in terms of size and location.

Therefore, new directions became necessary in the late seventies. The aim of replacing "slums" with public housing units was dropped. A major slum upgrading program was introduced. Standards were lowered in public housing schemes; serviced-site schemes and core-housing schemes became common. Housing schemes were not confined to the major cities but were implemented in urban (and rural) areas throughout the nation. The agency in charge of public housing schemes was decentralized into regional agencies. Tunisia's example should not be taken as a model, for many problems remain. There remains the fundamental problem of ensuring that public programs actually match the very diverse needs that are found within lower income groups--needs in terms of location, repayment scheduling, degree of self-construction demanded, size of plot, etc. A large shantytown has developed just beside the largest new low-income residential development in Tunis. The problem of quality control for the contractors used by the public housing agency remains--as in most other countries. But the understanding that major public intervention in the land market was a precondition of more successful "planning," that city governments must have the manpower and resources to plan effectively, and that standards should be more flexible ensures that Tunisia's program is and will be a lot more effective than those of most other Third World governments.

## PUBLIC INFRASTRUCTURE INVESTMENT

With limited budgets for investments in infrastructure, there are obvious trade-offs between meeting standards and reaching people. Such is the problem, for example, when inappropriate standards ensure that a small elite gets piped water and sewage while the poor get nothing. It is common throughout the Third World for high-income neighborhoods to have western water supplies while the poorest neighborhoods rely on water of dubious quality that costs ten to twenty times the "elite" price per liter. This concentration on high standards for the elite and little or nothing for the rest originated in colonial times--although vested interests have ensured that little has been done since to change it. Even today, the few urban areas in African and Asian countries with sewage systems were originally colonial enclaves that had sufficient Europeans to "justify" the construction of these systems.

Public health legislation and the subsidiary rules, bylaws, and codes that govern infrastructure standards are still a function of colonial standards established to provide for colonial elites. Or they are borrowed from western models established many decades ago in countries where very different conditions prevailed. Most of Kenya's public health controls are based on legislation passed in Britain more than a century ago. Kenyan legislation will not allow much in the way of alternatives to conventional waterborne sewage systems designed to traditional British standards.[18] Various ways of meeting basic health standards at low unit costs are not allowed. Septic tanks may be allowed, but not in plot sizes that low-income households can afford. Public health authorities are reluctant to relax standards embodied in the Public Health Act or in sanitation codes. The over-expensive standards simply ensure that the majority have no public provision for sanitation.

But the problem is not only one of cost. In many lower income residential areas, conventional waterborne sewage systems do not function efficiently. Since densities of occupation grow over time in many settlements, and since water consumption per capita is frequently low, there is often insufficient waste water to ensure that self-cleansing velocities are achieved in sewers. This is also a result of the lack of trained personnel in city and national governments with the knowledge to choose appropriate standards and technologies that will increase the number of people who have access to water and sanitation.

Of course, the provision of basic infrastructure and service is not only an issue of standards. It is also an issue of government support--i.e., the extent to which there are provision features in the development budget. Not surprisingly, infrastructure and service provision to lower income communities receives low priority. What is perhaps more surprising is that their provision also receives low priority from most aid agencies. Studies of multilateral aid flows showed that water and sanitation investments accounted for less than 5 percent of total multilateral aid from fifteen major agencies from the time the agencies began operations up to the late 1970s.[19] Additionally, city governments do not provide "illegal" settlements with water, sanitation, and basic services because they are illegal. As noted earlier, the inhabitants of these illegal settlements can make up one-third or more of an entire city's population. They play essential economic roles by providing the city with cheap labor, cheap goods, and cheap services. Yet their right to basic services is not accepted; even where basic services are provided, their quality and maintenance are often lacking.

**CONCLUSION**

In summary, then, cities provide one of the most visible manifestations of wealth and poverty. Differences in house size and quality between one district and another mirror their occupants' differences in wealth and income. Differences in infrastructure and service standards mirror differences in political power and influence. Differences in death rate, disease incidence, or infant mortality rates are of the most tangible indicators of income differentials.

Under the aegis of planning--in the controls imposed on private sector activities, in the positive actions taken by city government to tackle housing problems, and in the type of infrastructure investment program undertaken--there is a possibility of addressing one important aspect of this disparity--people's access to secure houses that meet minimum health and safety standards and provide basic services. In this context, preventive planning, i.e., planning whose aim is to prevent or lessen problems inherent in the search of lower income groups for adequate, healthy accommodation, is fundamental. As such, it can never be treated as a technical question. It involves guaranteeing low-income households access to cheap, legal house plots, changing the emphasis on standards from "controls" to technical advice, and devoting a higher proportion of investment to provision of lower income groups with improved infrastructure and services.

## NOTES

[1]M. Kaufman, The Housing of the Working Classes and
of the Poor, first published by T. C. and E. C. Jack
(London, 1907) and reprinted by EP Publishing (London,
1975), describes the proliferation of parliamentary acts
in Britain in the second half of the nineteenth century,
including the Common Lodging-Houses Act, the Labouring
Classes Lodging Act, the Nuisance Removal Act, the
Artisans' and Labourers' Dwellings Act, the Artisans'
Dwellings and Improvements Acts, the Working Classes
Act, and finally the Housing of the Working Classes Act
of 1890 (the most important one) that had supplementary
acts in 1893, 1894, 1896, 1900, and 1903.
[2]Lesley Doyal with Imogen Pennell, The Political
Economy of Health (London: Pluto Press, 1981).
[3]Charles E. Rosenberg, The Cholera Years (Chicago:
University of Chicago Press, 1962).
[4]Kaufman, Housing, passim.
[5]David Aradeon, "Southwest Nigeria," in Small and
Intermediate Urban Centres in the Third World: Their
Role in Regional and National Development, Jorge E.
Hardoy and David Satterthwaite, eds. (London: Hodder
and Stoughton, 1985), Chapter 6.
[6]Richard I. Lawless, "Social and Economic Change in
North African Medinas" in Change and Development in the
Middle East, eds. John I. Clark and Howard Bowen Jones
(London: Methuen, 1981), p. 266.
[7]Anthony D. King, Colonial Urban Development:
Culture, Social Power and Environment (London:
Routledge and Kegan Paul, 1976), pp. 267-268.
[8]Doyal, Political Economy.
[9]A. L. Mabogunje, J. E. Hardoy, and R. P. Misra,
"Shelter Provision in Developing Countries," Scope 11
(New York: John Wiley and Sons, 1978), p. 363.
[10]G. W. Kanyeihamba, "The Impact of the Received
Law on Planning and Development in Anglophonic Africa,"
International Journal of Urban and Regional Research 4,
no. 2 (June 1980).
[11]The Secretary of the Ministry of Justice under
Allende's government in Chile pointed to the contra-
diction between governments committed to improving lower
income groups' living conditions and operating within
legal channels designed by middle and upper income
groups to protect their own interests and maintain their
political power.
[12]Kanyeihamba, "Received Law."
[13]J. Courtney, Urban Land Policy Issues and
Opportunities, Volume II, World Bank Staff Working Paper
No. 283 (Washington, D. C.: World Bank, 1978), p. 129.
[14]To give some examples: in 1975, over 1 million
people were reported to live in temporary self-built
housing within the Bangkok-Thonburi municipal boundaries

58

in Thailand with no security of tenure or with very
short-term tenure agreements.  In Manila, in the Philippines, a 1978 report suggested that there was a total
of 328,000 squatter families with a total population of
close to 2 million inhabitants living in 415 sites
throughout the urban region. In Bombay, India, a survey
in 1975 found 560 squatter areas with about 1.3 million
people living in them. In Delhi, estimates suggest that
approximately 600,000 people live in squatter settlements while another 690,000 live in more than 300 hundred "unauthorized" colonies (essentially illegal subdivisions).  In Nairobi, Kenya, a 1978 estimate suggested
that 38 percent of the population lived in uncontrolled
and unauthorized settlements.  In Bangui, Central African Republic, three-fourths of the population live in
unofficial settlements in largely self-built housing. In
Guayaquil, Ecuador, a 1975 estimate suggested that 60
percent of the population live in "pirate" developments,
essentially illegal subdivisions, although over time
some of these have been legalized.  In Mexico City, at
least one-half of the population in the metropolitan
area lives in some form of uncontrolled settlement.
Comparable examples from most major Third World Cities
could be quoted.  In each instance, these communities
are largely self-constructed, virtually all have inse-
cure tenure, and virtually all have inadequate or no
basic services.  See Jorge E. Hardoy and David Satterthwaite, "Third World Cities and the Environment of Poverty," Geoforum 15, no. 3 (1984).

[15]Patrick McAuslan, Urban Land and Shelter for the
Poor, (London and Washington, D.C.: Earthscan, 1985),
passim.

[16]McAuslan, Urban Land.

[17]In this light, it is interesting to note the
experience in Cuba after 1959.  There, an emphasis on
potable water, sewers, health services, education, and
adequate diets has produced one of the highest life ex-
pectancies and lowest death rates in Latin America.

[18]Roger England, "Legislation Prevents Progress,"
unpublished paper, 1981.

[19]Silvia Blitzer, Jorge E. Hardoy, and David
Satterthwaite, "The Sectoral and Spatial Distribution of
Multilateral Aid for Human Settlements, Habitat
International, 7, no. 1/2 (1983).

# CHAPTER 3

# Preventive Education:
# Social Action and
# Community Self-Help

GUY W. STEUART

Education, in the commonly accepted sense of planned learning, has a significant role to play in the prevention of diseases and the promotion of health. Education for health, both "adult health education" as well as "school health education" for the school-attending population, can provide knowledge, influence attitudes, and facilitate behavior favorable to the prevention of diseases and the promotion of health. Education is, however, only a complementary function in a more global complex of health-related social and behavioral activities. Where programs have focused on education as the exclusive or prime determinant of social and behavioral change, they have rarely if ever come up to expectations. Even nonformal education, emerging from a disillusionment with more didactic styles and having as its foundation a learning process that is people- rather than instructor-centered, cannot claim on its own any striking successes, at least with respect to health status changes of populations. However, the potential role and contribution of the people themselves cannot be denied.

Health status is in fact a function of constitutional factors. It is also a function of the whole round of daily living that includes food- and water-related behavior; the protection or pollution of the physical environment; drinking; smoking; personal hygiene habits; the cycle of work, exercise, rest, recreation, and sleep; sexual behavior; behavior during pregnancy and delivery; and the care and rearing of chil-

dren. It is a function, too, of self-care and the dis-
criminating use of health and other human services to
the extent these are accessible. It is clearly a function of rural or urban living and, more decisively perhaps, of socioeconomic class. Finally, it is a function
of interpersonal relations in the social environment,
the reciprocal provision of emotional and instrumental
support, the ability to cope with stress, and general
competence in managing the normative problems of everyday life.

Broadly, then, health is to a critical extent a
function of social, cultural, and behavioral conditions
ranging from individual, kin and nonkin, local neighborhood, and community behavior to the behavior of
various levels of government, including not only
health policy as a whole as it affects the distribution
of goods, resources, services, and opportunities to the
population. Thus, while curative medical care may be
"delivered" by health services, what these services can
"deliver" with respect to prevention of diseases (notably, for example, through immunization or protection of
certain water and food supplies) is rather limited.

## THE DELIVERY-TEACHING STRATEGY

The curative clinical situation in which medicine is
most at home is characterized by the relative compati-
bility of the motives and priorities of the care-
provider role and the dependence of the client with
respect to diagnosis, treatment, and the prescription of
a self-care regimen. There is only peripheral involvement, if any, of other human services. Not unnaturally,
there is a strong tendency to extend this general model,
with some modification, to preventive and promotive
health programs for the public at large.

Thus in the preventive and promotive endeavor on
behalf of communities, the most common program strategy
is characterized almost exclusively by professional
diagnosis of the situation or problem, an epidemiological
"needs assessment," and the professional design and
implementation of the program solutions. At worst, only
lip-service is given to community views and roles. When
community views are actually surveyed and examined, they
are treated as obstacles to be overcome rather than
factors that might transform the planning, design,
application, and evaluation of a program. At best, the
"community" is co-opted into a program through the invi-
tation of those views that are likely to be supportive
of the professional plan. Thus, communities frequently
have a nominal rather than substantive and infusive
representation. The cooperation (read "compliance") of
the people is sought through teaching efforts that dis-
seminate information about health and behavior relation-

ships and that include exhortations to change behavior accordingly. There is commonly a heavy investment in mass media, because of their extensive reach, and in school health instruction, because this involves a captive and presumably susceptible population. Nonformal education that focuses on the learners' views, perceived needs, and priorities is singularly neglected, for reasons not the least of which is its implicit threat to professional control.

Programs tend as well to focus on categorical health and disease goals and almost exclusively on those that are organic in nature, with mental health (usually mental illness) either absent, neglected, or the entirely separate responsibility of psychiatric and mental health agencies. The focus is also on the individual and, to some extent, the family (most freqently the household) as the units of diagnosis and practice. Although the term "community" is commonly used, it is rarely more than a substitute term for "population." It is seen mainly as a geographically bounded aggregate of individuals and households and described primarily, if not exclusively, in quantitative demographic terms. Thus, although on occasion the community may be referred to as a "unit of practice," since it lacks the conceptual clarity and qualitative integrity of the notions of individual and of household, it is neither conceptually nor operationally analogous to them.

This general strategy usually does not meet the outcome expectations of programs, because it is implicitly and actually incompatible with the priorities of the people. This is so because at the preventive, and especially the health promotive, end of the intervention spectrum (unlike at the curative end), health maintenance simply does not dominate the daily needs, frustrations, and practical living problems of most people around the world. Health services frequently experience a clash between the culture of health professionals and the culture of the people they are attempting to serve.

It should be noted, however, that this strategy is not inevitably doomed to failure. Where the aims of the health service and of the people's priorities are compatible, where the expected behavior change does not demand a disruption of people's daily living needs and coping styles, and where such change is seen as eminently practical, it can be extraordinarily successful. Moreover, without deserting its general pattern of "deliver and teach," it can be and has been used effectively, particularly when it modifies "delivery" in the light of social and cultural realities. But this strategy's intrinsic assumption of shared professional and public needs and priorities remains a pervasive and serious limitation, a limitation exacerbated by the fact that most of the health needs of the Third World, at least, will be met in the longer run only through radical social change.

In summary, then, this general program pattern may be described as a managerial, social-control strategy directed toward correcting deviations from the elegant norms that constitute the health professional's view of what the world ought to be.

## THE PHYSICAL, MENTAL, AND SOCIAL NATURE OF HEALTH

To appreciate fully the need for a strategic alternative, we must reexamine the global nature of human health. Habitat and human environment refer not simply to the physical and biological but to the psychosocial as well. It is well-recognized that physical and social environments are not dichotomous. The "social diseases" of massive unemployment, overcrowding, migration and community uprooting, social disorganization, and the disruption of interpersonal support systems and sociocultural coping styles are all intimately associated with poor housing and slum conditions, pollution of the physical environment, water supply inadequacies, and therefore with severe physical environmental health hazards.

As Stewart Wolf points out, there is an investigative history of some considerable persuasion that contends a person's physical health and longevity are in part functions of the quality of his or her social adjustment. This notion, as he remarks, however, "has not been incorporated into the mainstream of biomedical scientific thought."[1] There is descriptive, epidemiological, experimental, and, indeed, clinical evidence supporting the notion that psychological adjustment is to a marked extent predictive of physical health status; that susceptibility to organic disease is increased under conditions of rapid social and cultural change; and that emotionally devastating events such as the death of a spouse or the loss of employment are organically pathogenic. As Wolf points out again, such evidence does not in any way reduce the significance of genetic and physical environmental factors as health determinants. But these factors contribute to health status in a synergistic rather than summative manner. He reviews as well the increasingly powerful, more particularized evidence of the mechanisms that mediate between the emotional and the physical and that provide the foundations for the more molar relationships observed between the physical, the mental, and the social health of studied populations.[2]

Add now to material Wolf has summarized the growing evidence from the field of mental health and psychiatry that mental health status, while to some extent dependent on constitutional makeup, is also a function

of (a) membership in social support systems that mitigate stress, (b) successful modes of coping with crisis, and (c) an everyday problem-solying competence
that precludes feelings of helplessness.

It would appear then that people's perception of
their social and physical environment and its emotional
impact upon them affects their susceptibility to organic
illness. Even if this were not so, such perception would
still have a significant impact on mental health status
in its own right. From a social and behavioral viewpoint then, while the overt behaviors of people in response to their physical and biological habitat are
critical to their health, so is their emotional adjustment to the physical, biological, and social environment.

It seems we need to consider seriously an alternative to the traditional "delivery-teaching" strategy,
one that would facilitate and enhance health-related
social and behavioral change outcomes. In the process,
interpersonal support systems, community integrity,
coping skills, and everyday problem-solving competence
might be strengthened and stabilized. Such a strategy
would, over time, aim to develop an increasingly active,
self-helping public that would not have to be stimulated
by external heroic efforts whenever new health-related
issues need solutions.


## COMMUNITY PROBLEM-SOLVING STRATEGY

In contrast to the more common managerial, profes-
sionally-dominated "delivery-teaching" or social control
model, we need to consider an alternative model, one
that an appreciable number, though still a small minority, of health services are tentatively exploring.
This alternative is a community-professional cooperation
model with a community-determined action thrust supported by professional consultation. Its implicit potential is social change rather than control.

It should be pointed out from the start that this
model does not exclude any of the more specific features
and procedures that characterize program development in
planning, needs assessment, design, or evaluation. But
it does place these in a different context, alters their
sequence, often changes their form, and demands additional procedures and processes. This community problem-
solving strategy is distinguished from the delivery-
teaching by several fundamental features.

First, the foundation, direction, and driving force
of the action rest less on the "outside" or etic view of
the intervening professionals than upon the "inside" or
emic view of the people themselves; their priorities,
expectations, and indigenous expertise are complemented
by professional support and consultation. It repre-

sents, therefore, an attempt from the start to establish community rather than professional control and "possession" of the program, to graft professional contributions onto the existing flow of motivation, and therefore, throughout the action, to avoid potential conflicts between the goals of the community and of the intervening professionals.

Second, professional designs and consultation are determined not only by the demographic features of the serviced population but by relatively well-defined notions of the psychosocial systems represented by individuals, kin groups, interpersonal networks, neighborhoods, larger communities, urban areas, rural regions, and ultimately, the nation. The approach toward these social units is made from the special point of view of potential actions within and by these social units. These actions are complementary to one another, are designed to meet the individual's and the community's perceived needs, and employ styles and techniques appropriate to their social and cultural makeup.

The aim of this approach is to enhance the potential for adaptive social change over which the people exercise some control and in which cooperative problem-solving is a function of strengthened support systems and occurs at a pace that does not disrupt continuity with the cultural past and present.

The units of practice in the proposed strategy are represented by those psychosocial systems or units conceptualized primarily from the emic viewpoint and complemented by the etic view of the intervening professional.[4] A social system or unit ("unit" in the sense of "unitary" rather than of "element") is a "unit of identity" to the extent that its members perceive themselves as sharing a common life experience, having mutual and reciprocal expectations of affective and instrumental support, having common priority needs and aspirations, and sharing a sense that the fate of one or more of the unit's members is a concern of all. The definition requires modification for the individual so that at the personal level there is a sense of identity, some level of personality integrity, and an absence of disabling emotional conflict.

At the same time, a social unit is a "unit of solution" to the extent that it can contribute through its own capability and efforts to the resolution of health-related problems. Thus to the extent a social unit is a unit of identity, it is also a unit of solution when it expresses and satisfies the emotional and mental health needs of its members, and meets elemental instrumental needs as well. Most social units of identity will, of course, have unrealized further potential as units of solution.

Units of identity and of solution are open, interacting systems with complementary roles that to various degrees may be compatible or incompatible with one another. There are few if any health-related problems that are not in part expressions of such interactions and whose solutions do not require mutually compatible purposive behavior by individuals, kin groups, neighborhoods, and larger social units, including governments. To the extent a unit of identity and a unit of solution, in respect to any defined health-related problem, are coterminous and isomorphic, there exists a necessary, if not sufficient, condition for the solution of that problem by the concerted efforts of the members themselves. This last feature is critical to the conceptualization and operation of health care programs.

Units of practice are simply those social units upon which a particular professional intervention may focus. Such interventions have at least two essential purposes that are fundamental to effective program action and that irrevocably bind together the processes and the outcomes of intervention. First, there is the strengthening of existing units of identity as social support systems so that they exercise a moderating influence on membership stress and enhance their own capability as units of solution through internally motivated action facilitated by professional consultation.

Second, there is the extension of existing units of identity, without weakening their own integrity, to embrace other units of identity and a broader membership so as to bring into play potentially more powerful units of solution. A prime example of this was the attempted extension by Martin Luther King, Jr., of the "black" unit of identity to embrace the "poor" of whatever ethnic background as a new unit of identity and of solution.

## GOAL RECOGNITION AND ORGANIZATION

The community-professional cooperation model is based on assessment of needs as the people define them. This includes but is not exclusive to health or health-directed needs. When only health (in the sense defined by professionals) or health-directed items constitute the burden of needs assessments, it is hardly surprising that the medical care of the sick or the provision of hospitals appear so frequently as priorities in the people's response. In contrast, a health-related, rather than health-directed, needs assessment that asks, "What is it like to live here?" will yield a somewhat different needs profile. When urban ghetto residents in large North American cities are asked these kinds of questions, they respond in terms of discrimination, police brutality, lack of safety in the streets, overcrowding, lack of employment, and a sense of hopelessness about the future. These factors are of consi-

derably greater significance for their general health,
both mental and physical, and for their stimulation into
self-help action, than the categorical epidemiological
priorities that health professionals so often present to
them.

But such priority needs do not exclude the
epidemiologically derived goals of health professionals.
It is in the nature of health and the ecology of its
determinants that when professionals have accurately
identified major health problems, these problems will be
intimately related to the many priorities expressed by
the people, (as identified by accurate needs assessment
methods). Categorical epidemiological priorites are not
irrelevant in and of themselves, but they commonly lack
the capacity to moticate people to critical and necessary action.

Wide-angle, health-related needs assessments, then,
provide three types of data that are of fundamental
importance for program action. They provide information
concerning aspects of living experience that are invariably of epidemiological significance for health status
even in the most narrowly defined medical terms. They
identify the major sources of stress relevant both to
physical well-being and to mental health. They also
identify the motivational and action potential of the
population of intended beneficiaries.

This general strategy when proposed almost inevitably gives rise to the question: what possible response can health services make if the people want something that health services cannot provide? This leads
in turn to the conclusion that while it may be desirable
to have the people participate to the greatest extent
possible, they should not be in a position to make
decisions with respect to priorities. This is of course
the typical authoritarian response of most human services and is justified on the grounds that professionals, not the people themselves, "know what's good
for them." Professionals, after all, have knowledge;
people only have beliefs.

If, however, the priority needs of the people and
those of health professionals are complementary, rather
than in conflict, then the critical art of the strategy
is the discernment of these complementary relationships,
some reorganization of professional goals, action by the
community to address selected goals of its own, and the
consultative grafting of categorical health objectives
onto such action as it gathers strength and momentum.
But the strategy also invariably demands that health
services establish close coordinative relationships with
a range of other human services so that by their joint
efforts community priorities may be addressed as nearly
as possible in the form in which those priorities were
expressed.

It should be stressed that the cooperative strategy
is based less on democratic idealism than it is on
pragmatic considerations arising from previous program
failures using traditional strategies. Moreover, the
strategy does not imply a passive professional role but
one of active persuasion and consultation. It demands
sophisticated skills additional to, and not excluding,
those skills necessary to the delivery-teaching strategy. Moreover, the strategy is as appropriate to a
specific program such as oral rehydration as it is to
more global health goals.

Finally, the strategy invariably embraces two broad
sets of goals. First, it aims to strengthen community
muscle and competence, support systems, and coping
styles in order to reduce stress; to enhance mental
health as well as its organic health correlates; and to
provide an increasingly strong foundation for future
programs. Second, it aims more directly to achieve
material and physical health outcomes including, for
example, improvement of dwelling units, the supply and
use of safe water, adequate sewage disposal and the like
that are the products of overt individual, kin group,
small group, community, and government action.


## HEALTH, HABITAT, AND THE INFORMAL SECTOR IN URBAN AREAS

A relevant example of this proposed strategy in less
developed countries, Africa in particular, is provided
by the life circumstances and needs of the "informal
sector" of urban populations. Mabogunje provides an
excellent analysis of this situation.[5] Industrialization, while attracting a significant proportion of the
most highly employable segments of rural populations, is
nonetheless able to employ only a small proportion of
them. The massive, "unemployed" informal sector that
includes self-employed individuals who may contrive to
achieve a fairly steady income, also includes a very
large number of people who have to scrape together a
living as best they can through petty trading, domestic
service, portering, crafts, theft, begging, and other
such means as may be available to them.

The housing needs of this informal sector pose
serious problems. There is a tendency for urban authorities to maintain strict housing standards, largely
derived from western countries, that have little or no
relationship to local resource availability and
practicality. It is not surprising, then, that governments report acute housing shortages: Mabogunje dis-
cusses a reported deficit of about 110 million dwelling
units in underdeveloped countries during the period
1960-1975.

For most members of this informal sector, the
practical solution is shelter self-construction using

readily available materials and squatting on vacant land
that might be available.  In the past thirty years,
there has been an increasing number of squatter settlements whose level of development, according to Mabogunje, reflects the degree of land tenure security that
squatters believe they have.  Governments, on the other
hand, seem constantly engaged in urban projects to evict
squatters that are instituted to improve the international public image of the city, or to ensure that
standards beyond the means of squatters are maintained,
or because the settlements are on prime development
land.  Thus, as Mabogunje points out, the squatters are
not thereby abolished.  They simply appear elsewhere.
As government moves in to evict, the squatters' con-
fidence and expectations are destroyed and, quite naturally, the squatters have no motivation to improve
dwelling construction or their environs in any new area
they may settle, so that the problem is perpetuated
rather than solved.

Moreover, the government provides few if any services, and people find themselves having to do the best
they can for water supply, refuse and sewage disposal,
and home and environmental maintainence. The spontaneous
development of these settlements with no orderly layout
leads particularly to refuse and sewage problems and,
generally, the degraded condition of much urban
development in the Third World. Mabogunje emphasizes
that one of the most significant problems of the urban
environment in underdeveloped countries is that these
large segments of the population lack a sense of
belonging to and of having a stake in the future of
their neighborhood and of the city.

He suggests that if urban administrations adopted a
more laissez-faire attitude, rather than engage in
periodic "clean-up" drives, such low-income groups might
be better off and would have a better opportunity to
develop their own communities and the social organization necessary to achieve them. In support of this view,
he points out further that areas of acute environmental
degradation are not necessarily areas of serious social
delinquency.  In this respect, it is interesting that
recent mental health literature frequently emphasizes
that emotional breakdown in such areas is less surprising than the extraordinary number of people who seem
to be able to manage under the most adverse environmental conditions.

The community problem-solving strategy that has
been proposed above, would seem singularly appropriate
with respect to the habitat and environmental concerns
of this urban informal sector.  It would involve efforts
to change urban government policy and attitudes and to
strengthen local squatter communities of identity and of
solution through health and human service collaboration
and stimulation of community self-help action.  It would

facilitate the extension of units of identity and of solution beyond tribal and other traditional community boundaries and would establish a sense of security and commitment to the welfare and future of individual neighborhoods as well as of the city as a whole.

## CONCLUSIONS

Education in the commonly accepted sense, whether it be formal or nonformal, without social action that involves both government support and self-help by the people is unlikely to achieve any desired changes. Education should occur as a function of social action rather than as a precursor of it. Even that most passive of educational settings, the school, should be part of the action. This can be achieved through the development of stronger links between school and community and greater participation by the community as a whole in school activities.

One of the problems that constantly surfaces in regard to education as a means of generating preventive or promotive action is that prevention and promotion are so "future-oriented" that they generate almost insurmountable motivational problems. The point, however, seems to be that education, particularly nonformal education, in an action-oriented context, can be very much "present-oriented" by addressing the immediate needs of the people and strengthening their sense of having a predictable future over which they have some control.

Health and human habitat problems, on the best evidence we have, have some prospect of solution on a step-by-step basis, however gradual, if governments can be persuaded to adopt more global, community participation strategies rather than the fragmented and sporadic efforts that too frequently characterize their approaches at present.

## NOTES

[1]Stewart Wolf, Social Environment and Health. (Seattle: University of Washington Press, 1981), passim.
[2]Wolf, Social Environment.
[3]Marc Kessler, and George W. Albee, "An Overview of the Literature of Primary Prevention," in G. W. Albee and J. M. Joffee, eds., Primary Prevention of Psychopathology, vol. 1. (Hanover, New Hampshire: University Press of New England, 1977), pp. 351-399.
[4]Guy W. Steuart, "The People: Motivation, Education and Action." Bulletin of the New York Academy of Medicine, Second Series, 51, no. 1 (January 1975):174-185; Guy W. Steuart, "Psychosocial Bases of Behavior

Change," in Communication and Behavior Change, Proceedings of the VIIth International Conference on Health and Health Education, Buenos Aires, 1969, published in International Journal of Health Education, Part IV, 427-442; Guy W. Steuart, "Social and Cultural Perspectives: Community Intervention and Mental Health," in Perspectives in Primary Prevention, Proceedings of the Fourteenth Annual John W. Umstead Series of Distinguished Lectures, February 8-9, 1978, North Carolina Division on Mental Health and Mental Retardation Services, Raleigh, North Carolina, pp. 145-163.

[5]Akin L. Mabogunje, The Development Process: A Spatial Perspective. (London: Hutchinson University Library for Africa, 1980), pp. 181-198.

# Discussion

Lacey: You refer to the social change agent as the health person, the health educator, who's going to help mobilize the community. How does one keep the process going once the social change agent has left?

Steuart: I don't know how you do that. What I suspect, however, is that, as a general rule, if one adopts the rather simple principle of not doing anything the community could not conceivably do for itself without your assistance, survival is more likely to occur. One of the successes that we had in the Cameroon project, a USAID effort that combined community development and personnel training, was in a multiethnic settlement. There were a number of these multiethnic settings, so it was impossible to start at the level of organization that would have required all of the groups to collaborate. So we worked initially with the separate units of identity, largely in an unstructured way, to help them to conduct an examination of their own section of the community in terms of what they felt the priority needs were, regardless of health. As they began to address these problems—and there were major environmental problems that they did in fact raise quite spontaneously themselves—they began to move to larger units of solution, so that after some period of time, in two or three of these remote villages, the separate ethnic groups had made their own decisions to step up the collaborative council designed to act on behalf of all three, because they were attempting to address problems that they recognized each individual unit could not address on its own.

Donahue: Six or eight years ago the Philippine government moved people out of an area to resettlement

71

camps about forty or fifty kilometers outside of the
city. What's now functioning there is a self-sustained
primary health care program that meets the basic health
service needs of this community of fifty thousand
people. The only government presence in the health sector seems to be a small health clinic that is basically
an in-building service. It was primarily accomplished by
the efforts of a really effective voluntary organization
that had a lot of experience in rural primary health
care organizational training. In the Philippines, you
have a large-scale, politically motivated, effective
community organization network, a loose one but very
powerful. The trainers are community women--it's mostly
all operated by women. The only professionals that have
some form of permanent involvement are two nurses. The
whole operation is done on a community basis, including
the basic first encounter diagnosis. They hardly ever
have a doctor appear. I didn't really answer how you
make sure these things happen, but I think an organization must have some vested interest. It must go beyond
the narrow project focus.

Steuart: I think that the delay in reaching a self-
generating momentum is largely a consequence of early
missteps in terms of delivery, rather than in getting
the community to act where it is capable of acting.
There is always impatience on the part of professionals
to deliver what they can and not to wait for the demand
for it to be generated or for a partial solution to be
offered by the community. The Papago Indians in the
United States are an interesting example of this, because they refused to accept federal health insurance.
In fact, they are the only Indian group I know of in
this country that both hire and fire the health personnel and create all the health programs on the reser-
vation. They were one of the pioneers in moving Indian
health services to the control of Indian health direc-
tors and personnel, who are not necessarily physicians.

Lacey: David Satterthwaite seemed to focus on the
reeducation of planners, the retraining of planners to
deal with the problems of improving health and housing
in developing countries and in cities in developing
countries. As a planning educator, how can planning education be changed to deal with health and housing in
developing countries, since in some respects we are part
of the problem?

Satterthwaite: It was arrogant of me to talk about
how to retrain planners. I am not a planner. I have had
some experience with the problems, and what I tried to
do was to outline the problems. Maybe it needs a much
more focused understanding of what we're trying to
address--what is planning trying to achieve? Having stated the goals, then a better understanding of how cities
form and function in the Third World would give you an
idea of where you can intervene.

Lacey:   In the 1960s, we got into advocacy planning, we got into societal learning models, and now the
latest phase is probably radical planning, which is trying to bring about structural change.  If there are new
roles for planners in cities in developing countries,
what should they be?   Where should we be going as a
profession in developing countries?  They are trying to
set up a planning curriculum in some universities in
Nigeria where I have worked.  Should they be focusing on
importing western education?  Should they try to develop
their own curriculum to deal with the problems?  You may
not be a planner, but you've travelled throughout a number of countries, and you know what some of the problems
are.

Satterthwaite:   I learned very little from planning
methodology in my own postgraduate training.  I learned
an awful lot from people who taught me analysis of what
caused what we saw.  And so, if you can begin to understand what is causing what is happening, then you can
begin to suggest where, as a planner, you can intervene.
Presumably, that's the best basis for any curriculum.

Moser:   But the process of education does not and
ought not to go only in one direction.  For example, the
term "informal sector" has been used here.   That is a
concept that came out of Third World planning and the
recognition of what was actually happening to people.
It was very difficult for poor people to get employment
for regular wages in the Third World.  We now have politicians in Britain using this term to describe the
Black colliery.  Also, some of us in Britain believe we
are learning more from the Third World about infla-
tionary economics than we can teach them.  In fact, in
some fields, we recognize that the Third World experience is more advanced, more valid than ours.

Donahue:   The kind of thing that I see done at
Asian School of Technology, I think, is really effective.  They tend to bring people from agencies in countries in Asia that have paid their dues to the system in
different low- to middle-level responsibilities.  They
come on a part-time basis. They work half-time back
where they came from, doing whatever it is they do, but
within the discipline of the education program, and the
other half of the time they spend learning together at
the university with some guidance from competent,
experienced, international people who know Asia well.
It seems to me to be a pretty effective way to try and
get at specific questions within a regional context,
because you're able to introduce all those useful things
that come out of planning training in North America  and
Europe--methodology and nuts and bolts--but you're
training within the context of the problems and the reality in which these people have to live, work, survive,
go back, and flourish.

Rohe: We owe Steuart a debt of gratitude for broadening our purview here in a number of respects. First, he has focused on the importance of the social environment as opposed to the physical environment. Over the last two days, the emphasis here has been on the relationship between the physical environment and physical health. He has brought in a whole new avenue for discussion--the importance of social structure characteristics. Second, he has alerted us to the importance of considering mental health and its connections to physical health. Both Steuart and Satterthwaite also emphasize the importance of land tenure in maintaining a strong social structure and the kind of incentives that are necessary for people to become involved in self-help programs. I think Satterthwaite's emphasis on unrealistically stringent housing standards is well-taken. The question becomes, however, do we throw out these standards completely, or can we somehow work with them, tone them down, alter them to make them more relevant for people in Third World countries? Can we make them more flexible to account for differences among countries, as well as among regions within countries? My sense is that we should not throw them out totally, but develop more realistic standards.

Should we have minimum standards, and if so, how can they be defined? Whether standards make sense at all depends on the answer to two questions. Is there some mechanism for enforcing the standards? Obviously, if there is no enforcement mechanism, or if the local government is not willing to expend the time and effort to enforce these standards, it is counterproductive to be talking about setting standards in the first place. Second, will bigger problems be caused by enforcing the standards--that is, by evicting people, bulldozing squatter villages, and so forth--than are being solved with the standards? One way to adapt the standards to Third World countries while maintaining some notion of a negative sanction or enforced standard would be to delegate responsibility for enforcement to a community group, if in fact one exists, rather than to state officials. Setting standards that are realistic for a particular locale should be done by negotiation between the local officials and local residents in terms of what they see as important, what they are willing to accept. They should be seen as one step up from existing conditions, not as an attempt to solve the problem immediately. There must be a certain amount of flexibility to account for individual variation as well as variation among regions. Enforcement should also be done in conjunction with certain positive incentives--like the provision of building materials at cost or at subsidized rates. Thus, if you are going to establish base line building codes, the necessary means for people to meet those building codes should be provided.

Western building codes and regulations tend to be concerned with things like building materials, design, size, setback, and so forth. My feeling is that those tend to be secondary concerns in Third World countries, where the focus should be on density. Most of the problems under discussion here are more closely related to density than to any other aspect of building: you cannot have pit privies if the density is extremely high. Contagious diseases are much more likely to be transmitted in very dense environments, etc. This causes immediate problems because the higher density environments are usually the areas with the least public services, and the maximum density at which health problems will occur will depend on the level of services provided to that area. For example, if you have running water, piped sewerage, and so forth, you can go to higher densities and not have the same health problems that you would expect at lower densities without those services. The issue, then, is how to assure that in areas without adequate services the density is kept low enough to accommodate or to ameliorate the kinds of problems that emerge in higher density areas. There is a need for some kind of land reform where individuals are leased plots at some rate they can afford, and along with that lease go certain stipulations that maintain and enforce density standards.

The last point has to do with the emphasis in Satterthwaite's paper on housing in urban areas. We must also focus on the countryside. If not, the appearance of low-cost housing in urban areas may precipitate the migration of rural people into the city and give rise to another round of the same problems.

Satterthwaite: Unfortunately, it is too simple to say that giving tenure to squatters is the answer. Giving tenure to squatters can commercialize the illegal land market, and the poor may get pushed out. For example, in Ankara, almost in desperation, the government after the fact acknowledged that if a squatter got onto the land and was still there the next morning with something like a housing structure, he could stay there. Basically, the government in Ankara in the 1960s accepted that if the police couldn't find the squatter before he was actually there with a basic housing structure, he could stay there, and the courts supported this. Thus, the lowest income groups had access to good land near the city center. However, later the "big boys" moved in and built small houses, three- or four-story walkups, and sold them to the middle class, who were finding the inner city of Ankara very congested. So yes, tenure is of great importance for low-income groups, but if you simply grant tenure as policy after the event, you will find that the financial interests in the official land market very quickly take over control of the unofficial land market.

As for standards, it would be nice for negotiations to take place between state officials and a community group, but the logistics would be very difficult. In many low-income areas, there are all sorts of people competing for power, prestige, whatever. It is a mistake to assume that low-income communities are homogeneous. In Tunis, for example, it was decided to legalize the squatter area. When they got down to the mechanism of doing so, they discovered that the early squatters had persuaded brothers, sons, cousins, uncles, and aunts to stake out some land that they then simply rented out to someone else. So, many of the people who got land originally in the squatter invasion in Tunis were actually people who were quite well off, who simply left their existing houses, squatted, demanded tenure over time, and were making a fortune out of it. So when you get down to the actual intervention, it is never quite so simple.

I do not think most of the health problems are related as much to density as to poverty, lack of income, not enough food, water, and sanitation. Of course, there is some correlation with density, but the problems occur because no alternative exists. To deal with the problem, you must provide more healthy alternatives that people can afford.

On the point of cheap housing encouraging migration to cities, the worst housing conditions in the world have not discouraged migration to the cities, why should good housing encourage it? In other words, housing quality does not seem to be linked to migration. Migration is essentially economic in nature. In rural areas, access to land is much easier. There, presumably, the problem is getting water and sanitation and primary health care--that's your housing strategy, not intervention into the building process.

Alonso: It seems to me that the problem that both urban planning and health have as disciplines is that by degrees you can incorporate the universe into your realm. So then we say the trouble with health is not so much disease per se, but it's poverty, unemployment, structure of society, and what we need to do is organize the community, to have land reform, and so on, and pretty soon you're restructuring the universe around your concern. In other words, the difficult thing is to find the bounds of an effective participation. In order to transform the economic basis of the society, you need to be a political leader or a revolutionary, not a health professional or a technical city planner. I'm not saying therefore that you can do nothing or very little, but you must define the realm in which you operate.

Crumley: You correlated western notions of zoning codes and setback and whatnot with density, and you seemed to give the impression that density could be measured quantitatively and that it was a question that could be affected technologically. The more important question might be one of cultural differences, because density is culturally determined, and the reactions to density are culturally determined--we can pack Japanese in closer than we can pack Swedes, etc. It seems to me that the proper role for ethnographic, historical, and ecological analyses is at the preplanning stage. Every society, formally and informally, has zoning codes, if you look at it that way. A Moslem household looks a certain way. If you're going to build houses for Moslems, it's to your advantage to look at what Moslem households have looked like for the last 20 years or the last 1000 years. It's to your advantage to see how Moslems view their ecological circumstances. If we took an ethnographic and historical beginning approach to working out a code appropriate to that place on the earth, then we'd get ourselves out of two problems:  the failure of the standard export of programs outside of a western context, and the ethical embarrassment of finding ourselves exporting western culture to Third World countries.

Rohe:  Yes, I agree with what you're saying. Though I'd even go one step further to say, not only do you need those kinds of studies, but you also need the people involved directly in negotiating those standards. One of my suggestions here is that you actually negotiate those with the community. The standards are not applicable everywhere. In some cases, the enforcement potential does not exist, or the community truly feels that these standards are not in their best interests. But I suspect in many instances, a community group would in fact like to become involved in a process of codifying some informal norms and values that have in fact developed over the years. You can help to reinforce those by making them more official and by clarifying them so that everybody understands that the community in that sense is in fact enforcing the housing codes.

Crumley:  The critical thing is not that everyone in the community understands those codes, it's that you understand those codes. They can implicitly understand those codes and go about building their houses just fine, thank you. The only reason that it needs to be explicit is if there's some intervention on the part of outside people who need spelled out to them exactly what that community's structures are. In that regard, it seems that our experience ought to be a learning one rather than a teaching one. We have to go into those communities and learn what those boundaries are and then negotiate the modification of those standards to improve health conditions.

Tulchin:  Most of the conversation this afternoon centered on planners and planning, intervention in planning, definition of community, points of entry for the planner, the role of the planner. Absent, to me as

a lay person in this field, has been discussion on the
part of health professionals on the question of how
health professionals, trained within a very rigid,
allotropic, positivist paradigm, cope with the individual and professional trauma of dealing with areas of
the world, the Third World particularly, where that
paradigm may not immediately be applicable. We've talked
here today about reactions within the discipline of
planning. The simple answer, in some form, has been to
infuse the study of planning with a Third World experience. My question would be, what is the analogy in
the health fields? Is there a Third World experience in
constructing a water supply? Is there a Third World
experience in medicine? Health delivery--perhaps. But
how do you adapt, if you can at all, the training, delivery, allotropic paradigm that dominates so much of
American medicine, particularly in its high-technology
forms.

# CHAPTER 4

# Planning for Preventive Medicine and Primary Care Medicine: Issues of Method and Habitat

DONALD L. MADISON, M.D.

Preventive medicine--as distinct from public health--is more a way of thinking than a way of doing. Clinical medicine is a way of doing that on the basis of its record tends to shortchange the preventive side.

Primary care medicine is clinical medicine at the general, nonhighly specialized level. It serves in any community as the entry level of clinical medicine. Its potential for preventive action is great--much greater than any other level of clinical medicine--but is largely unrealized. The reasons why this is so are partly attitudinal--on the part of the medical profession, in the way physicians are trained and, therefore, in the way they think and behave; partly organizational--at the point of local service delivery; and partly strategic-- in the way governments plan or fail to plan for primary care.

Primary care medicine is distinct, again, from primary health care as defined by WHO and UNICEF at the 1978 Alma Ata Conference. The primary health care as defined at Alma Ata included primary care medicine as one component in a list of basic services (health education, food and proper nutrition, safe water, basic sanitation, maternal and child health care, family planning, immunization against major infectious diseases, prevention and control of endemic diseases, treatment of common diseases and injuries, provision of essential drugs), both personal and environmental, most of them preventive. This definition also includes the most basic services necessary for health. If the concept has a weakness, it is that it represents a list of services;

it doesn't speak to their organization as a program and
only minimally to their relationship to each other.

## FOUR LEVELS OF PRIMARY CARE PLANNING

It is in primary care medicine that medicine's contribution to the prevention of poor health at the community
level is most likely, and it is usually at the primary
care level that profitable interactions between medical
personnel and habitat specialists occur. There are four
degrees or levels of planning specificity that units of
government have used in regard to primary care medicine.
The first and lowest level is merely to plan for
production of the necessary manpower resources and do
nothing else. This is the level of planning for primary
care that we use for the most part in the United States.
It is, essentially, an attempt to assure that a population will have sufficient numbers of primary care physicians, nurses, dentists, etc., and it presumably also
serves to protect us against a relative overabundance of
medical specialists as well as engineers, merchants,
teachers, clergymen, or anything else that young people
might aspire to become. Other industrialized nations use
it, too, but perhaps none with such great enthusiasm as
the United States. For many years, most Third World
nations did not think very far beyond this level either,
which meant that they concentrated on developing medical
schools and other training programs and left the diffu-
sion of the products of these institutions to chance.
One result of having limited the planning of primary
care to this first level is the differential in medical
manpower distribution between more attractive and less
attractive habitats (e.g., urban and rural, suburbs and
inner city). In the Third World, the result is seen
typically in the variance of physician distribution between the capital city and the rest of a country, and
for some nations in the physician emigration rates.
The second level of primary care planning adds to
the mere production of manpower resources (control of
overall supply) additional measures intended to guide
the geographic distribution of manpower resources: for
example, financial incentives to encourage the settlement of physicians and other health workers in resource-
poor areas, or negative incentives like the one used in
the United Kingdom. There, certain areas that are well-
supplied with physicians are "closed" to new general
practitioners under the National Health Service. Conscription and indirect conscription are the more direct
tactics for guiding distribution of manpower resources,
as is the limited term service obligation that many
governments impose on physicians in return for a public
or publicly supported medical education. A less direct
measure, falling between the first and second level, is

the strategy of opening new "regional" medical schools in resource-poor areas. This is based on the unproven assumption that the locus of medical education influences subsequent physician settlement.

This second level of primary care planning assumes (a) the existence of some source of economic support for the practitioners who locate in the targeted areas (for example, a national health service as in the United Kingdom, or the presumed ability of most people in the area to pay for the services they receive, as in the United States); and (b) a willingness and capability on the part of the practitioners to organize and operate a service that will correspond roughly to the settlement patterns of people. In practice, most of the strategies at this level are very inexact, and their overall record at solving the problems of primary care medicine, even of maldistribution of resources, is not good.

The third level adds to the first two the distribution and organization of primary medical services. It does not leave the arrangement of services to the whim of the doctors and other personnel, but instead actually guides their development and determines locations and configuration (of personnel, facilities, equipment, and so on) as well as specific operational guidelines. This implies sectorization, or if not sectorization, at least a population-based plan. This third level is followed in all socialist countries and in some nonsocialist industrialized and Third World countries. To a very small extent, it exists in the United States-- for example, primary medical care for Native Americans living on reservations is planned at this level, as is service to the enrolled members of prepaid group practice plans.

If health and habitat are to be seen at all as interdependent and, therefore, to be planned in concert, a fourth and higher level of primary care planning is necessary. This is a level that goes the next step beyond the planning of primary medical services to the planning of community health programs. There is an important difference between the two. A medical service assumes a general need for itself; a community health program follows the discovery of a specific need.

One problem with stopping at the third level of primary medical care planning is that the population is left with a service that will equal the dominant profession's view of what is most important. The physician's _raison d'être_ is the relief of pain and discomfort as experienced by individuals. This has always been true, not just of physicians but of all "healers." Ever since the birth of the university in the west in the late Middle Ages, the accepted medical method for dealing with pain and discomfort has been to investigate and treat the underlying disease--in each patient, one on one, one by one. Toward the end of the nineteenth century, the medical method began to demonstrate its superiority over other ways of healing. For the last fifty years, it has proven itself extremely effective, so much so that a failure to behave in this way now, an absence of this process in any community of people, is considered by most societies as a serious, perhaps the most serious, community health problem.

Yet an excess of attention to the medical method might also be a health problem for many communities, in this sense: when practicing physicians are left in charge of planning health services, their professional tradition and training shape what those services will look like, as well as what the demands for additional resources will be. Left to their own designs, medical services have a tendency to grow in size and complexity, looking only at the requirements of the immediate clinical case, unquestioning of the greater social payoff. The problem is that many health conditions requiring medical attention and interpretation do not lend themselves efficiently or effectively to the kinds of solutions that physicians automatically consider. The marginal payoff in improved health of the population from additional medical resources, once a basic medical service is in place, is likely to be much lower than it would be if some other personal health strategy were in place. For these reasons, stopping at the third level (planning medical services) is apt to become extraordinarily expensive, far too expensive for less developed countries.

The fourth level of primary care planning--planning health programs--goes beyond sectorization and other population-based constructs for medical service planning to an investigation not just of the shape and size of the population contained in the habitat but of the health problems that affect that population.

In stressing the limitations of the third level-- planning for primary medical services without going the next step to planning health programs--I have stressed the shortcomings of medical care. Yet I do not wish to imply that community health programs are in any way a substitute for primary medical services, nor that they should operate in addition to and apart from primary medical care. In fact, planning community health programs separate from medical services may be just as limiting. Except for instances where some particular disease or condition is extremely prevalent and likely to remain so for a considerable time, and therefore some justification exists for launching an all-out effort to control that particular problem, disease-targeted programs generally suffer from their lack of integration with a source of general medical services. This is so because on a local level the observations of primary care practitioners are often the best initial source of intelligence for community problems identification, and also because practitioners can be valuable program leaders and participants. Moreover, their records constitute a major repository of data necessary to measure results. Beyond this, one must keep in mind that people do not usually sort their own health problems into the categories that public health authorities often use. Therefore, they need a general dispensary they can identify as a source of undifferentiated health care, a dispensary that will treat the illness of anyone who seeks help, and that can at the same time organize special programs for those problems that affect groups of people--the entire community as well as certain subsets of it, problems that are best dealt with through group measures. In other words, the fourth level of primary care planning builds onto the third one by enlarging the traditional horizons of the primary care practitioner from the strictly clinical to the epidemiological and community aspects of care.

## COMMUNITY ORIENTED PRIMARY CARE

This is not a new concept. It has, however, recently been given great attention and a new name, "community oriented primary care" (COPC). COPC represents both an attitude and a method without which primary care medicine, whether sectorized or not, will never achieve its potential for improving a community's health either through cure or prevention. The concept's father figure was Dr. John Grant. He worked all over the world during his forty-two years with the Rockefeller Foundation promoting a type of institution that he called simply a "health center." Grant worked mostly in China, India, and Puerto Rico, but his influence was much wider than that.

Shortly after World War II, a group of health workers in South Africa advanced the concept further. Encouraged by the election of a progressive government, and drawing on Grant's ideas, the South African group organized the Institute of Family and Community Health in Durban. They subsequently opened several COPC centers in urban and rural communities, and the experience of these centers added significantly to Grant's basic model. Their major contribution to Grant's model was the idea of "community diagnosis" from a primary care setting: epidemiological investigation was extended and applied to communicable disease outbreaks and the search for cause in chronic disease, the measurement of a local community's health status and general well-being, and the direct application of the results to the design of specific interventions in the community. The South African centers also placed a strong emphasis on community participation, both in priority setting and as a source of information. They also used indigenous health workers as outreach members of the primary care team. The South African experience was a brief one because the government and its policy changed again after a short time, but the group's influence was, like Grant's, worldwide. Many of the group's members ultimately came to the United States, especially to Chapel Hill, where Sidney Kark--who coined the term Community Oriented Primary Care--and John Cassell were both chairmen of the Department of Epidemiology, and Guy Steuart became chairman of Health Education here at the University of North Carolina at Chapel Hill. Kark subsequently emigrated to Israel, where he continued to experiment with COPC. Cecil Slome, Eva Salber, and Harry Phillips were other Chapel Hill members of the South African group.

In the late 1960s, as part of President Lyndon Johnson's "War on Poverty," a national program of neighborhood health centers was developed for the United States. These centers were organized under guidelines that were largely inspired by Grant's model and the South Africa experience. The polyclinics that are the basic medical care units in Cuba, and that were at first operated only as medical service centers, began to implement COPC a few years ago. They use staffing and program guidelines and operate in a style that resembles very closely the Institute of Family and Community Health and the neighborhood health centers of the late 1960s in this country. There are many other examples of COPC around the world.

Recently, an American conference organized by the Institute of Medicine devoted itself to the COPC idea. One of the results of the conference was a generic definition of COPC. By "generic," I mean that any primary care medical practice, program, institution, or organization, of whatever configuration, size, location, or sponsorship can be said to be doing COPC when it acknowledges and applies the following five elements: (a) the clinical practice of primary medical care; (b) a diagnosis by the practice of the health problems for its community, using epidemiological methods (along with simple observation and intuition); (c) a means of soliciting and using the concerns, opinions, and observations of members of the community being cared for; (d) the implementation of such programs of care, information, and other community health actions as are suggested by the intelligence the practice has gathered; and (e) a continuing surveillance of the community's health and an evaluation of the practice's programs using an epidemiological approach, and an application of the results, as in a feedback loop, to further change.

This is, of course, an oversimplification. Nevertheless, these elements suggest some of the points where the interests of health care planners and habitat planners naturally intersect. Adopting a COPC strategy implies investment in a type of personal health services institution that uses planning and evaluation on a decentralized, individual program level in much the same way as other public institutions, e.g., education, law enforcement, transportation. Since the focus of its planning efforts, of its "community diagnosis," is the health status of the community, it considers the full range of health action, from prevention to cure to rehabilitation, as relevant to its program. This then tends to force interaction with other, nonpersonal health sectors.

Are COPC and the primary health care (PHC) of Alma Ata the same thing? Yes and no. The component services of PHC are basic. An absence of one of them in any community of people would by the COPC approach probably be cause for action, for implementation of the missing component. Yet PHC is a world "community diagnosis," a standard. Local communities differ in terms of their unique problems and in terms of priorities. COPC is an approach to any specific community; it implies organization and minimal fragmentation of effort. It is, therefore, a way of implementing primary health care using local priorities and local intelligence to design the individual programs of PHC and make them accountable to local situations. COPC is then not an alternative to PHC, but a locally responsive way of implementing it.

Since this discussion of primary care planning began from the medical point of view, I will finish with some thoughts about COPC from the medical view. First, COPC is comprised of any alliance between population-based precepts that have been the domain of public health and personal health care, as represented by primary care medicine. Second, COPC is particularly well-suited for Third World countries. Yet it is applicable anywhere. While it is true that "pluralistic," non-hierarchical systems of health services are not entirely in accord with the formally defined populations that a strict interpretation of the COPC model envisions, physicians, nurses, barefoot doctors, and all other primary care practitioners working in almost all settings have (or could have) a definition of the population for whom they care.

In an immediate and practical sense, COPC promises to make any primary medical service setting more effective. Although physicians over the years have tended to wait to see what comes to their door for treatment, this has never been an effective way of treating, let alone preventing, disease. This approach, and the training that leads to it, has never made clinicians particularly skilled with or interested in the population as a whole. COPC poses a paradigm that will enable a primary medical setting to analyze illness in the community and work in a prospective fashion to treat it. The issues may be as diverse as infant diar-

rhea or workplace safety, hypertension or hunger, long-
term care of the elderly or teenage pregnancy. The
possible interventions are equally diverse: public
education and case-finding, programs of support for the
families of stroke victims, water supply, organized
programs of latrine digging, screen installation, and
house-fire protection. The technique of community diagnosis followed by clinical and community action promises
an effectiveness that one-to-one treatment room medicine
cannot. Moreover, the COPC approach invites, actually
mandates, the involvement of the community in both diagnosis and treatment and, as such, builds community re-
sponsiveness into a primary medical service setting in a
manner that traditional medical practice does not. It is
a discipline and a method that requires step-by-step
communication with and involvement of the citizens of a
practice, the citizens of a community, and those who articulate the community's concerns for other nonmedical
but health-related areas. This distinguishes COPC from
the service of traditional medicine not only in its
clinical activities, but in its ethos.

There are of course many problems to be overcome--
problems of program organization, training of leaders
and workers, professional tradition, financing, politics, and others. Experience tells us what they are.
But the approach has much to commend it, and the few
instances in which it has been fully developed are among
the most successful examples of community health planning and effective health programs that we know of.

# CHAPTER 5

# Setting Priorities for Health Care

## C. ARDEN MILLER

Research that attempts to enlighten the relationship between health and other circumstances, such as habitation, is burdened by poor understanding of health as a measurable concept. My purpose here is to suggest ways that health can be measured in order that we may consider interventions that show the most promise for achieving, on behalf of a population, an improved level of health. This approach does not consider all possible definitions of health nor all ways to measure it. Scholarship in this field is extensive but not so definitive as to be presented in a way that is both succinct and free of bias.

The traditional medical view regards health as a kind of mystical, sublime state that must be protected insofar as possible from assault by toxins, poisons, germs, or accidents--insults that disrupt the sublime state. The medical view holds that if we understand those insults, and the body's response to them, then we can provide interventions in the form of cures that protect or restore the mystical state of perfection. That view of health needs to be understood and, probably, quickly discarded. It is a view that will not be helpful in the search to understand the reciprocal interactions between health and habitation. We seek more prevention. We seek to understand ways that health can be protected by understanding, and possibly intervening in, the physical and social environments that interact with the functioning of population groups.

A useful approach regards health in terms of adaptation. Good health represents a state of more or less successful adaptation to both social and physical

87

environments, recognizing that adaptation is a dynamic
state. All groups to some degree and from one time to
another suffer from some disequilibrium of adaptation.
That disequilibrium may be regarded as dis-ease. This
brings us to the traditional public health triad of
interactions: a host population, a physical environment, and a social environment, all of them interactive
with each other (see Figure 5.1).

FIGURE 5.1. Triad of Interaction

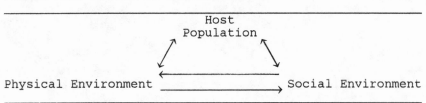

The model is useful in illustrating that the
physical environment can influence directly the health
of a population. For example, using Dr. Caroline Moser's
community case study of a squatter settlement in Guayaquil, unprotected walkways allow toddlers to fall into
and drown in the low water in which the shacks have been
erected.[1] In this situation, a host population could
increase its protection by filling in the swamp around
the shacks, a favorable change in the environment.
Interactions between environment and population may be
mediated through social organization. For example, in
the Guayaquil study, community organization was required
to improve the environment by acquiring a convenient
supply of potable water. Under other circumstances, social organization can threaten health, as when youth
gangs represent a hazard to the population.
    The model in Figure 5.1 accentuates the multiple
causality of disease. Interesting reports dating from
World War II concentration camps suggest that rates of
tuberculosis in those camps varied inversely with the
amount of protein that was available in the diet. Does
this mean that tuberculosis is caused by poor diet? In
a sense it does. The presence of a germ in the environment may be a necessary condition for "causing" tuberculosis. But that cause does not become operational unless a variety of other causes are also brought to bear.
    The model also suggests caution about interventions
that are designed to improve health. Well-intentioned
tinkering with one apex of the triangle may produce un-
expectedly adverse consequences elsewhere, such as
happened in the Pruitt-Igoe projects.[2] Those sanitized
housing developments were designed to improve the interaction between host and physical environment but destroyed the social structure that was even more protective than the physical environment. Vulnerable popu-

lations suffered from disastrous maladaptations to stress, violence, and isolation.

Regarding health as a dynamic state of adaptation requires us to look at disease in terms of multiple causality. It also requires us to look at cures and promising interventions in a variety of ways. In this volume, H. M. Misra presents an interesting example of an Indian village where many small infants die in the first year of life from infantile tetanus. That health problem, as with many others of that village, might be addressed by means of substantial social reform and income redistribution. A good case can be made for that approach. A good case could also be made for going into the village, working with the traditional midwife, and immunizing pregnant women against tetanus. Another approach would intervene with the physical environment and prevent tetanus by separating animals from people. Each of these three approaches enjoys a plausible rationale; each intervenes at a different apex of the triangle.

The multiple factors that contribute to disease must be examined in their full context and decisions made about the interventions that are most appropriate to local circumstances. Generalizations about the most promising approaches are simply not possible without community diagnosis and decisionmaking in which the community itself gives guidance on approaches that are both feasible and acceptable. With an emphasis on health as a state of more or less satisfactory adaptation to physical and social environment, it may be possible to suggest a system of priorities that promise to foster or promote successful adaptation.

Figure 5.2 and the comments that follow deal only with issues of maternal and child health, a defensible emphasis for most Third World nations. The priorities in Figure 5.2 were prepared nearly a decade ago with the guidance of Dr. Jessie Bierman, for many years the Maternal and Child Health Director of WHO. As with all generalizations, this scheme will not be appropriate in every specific situation. A scheme unique to local circumstances would need to be prepared. Still, the priorities provide a generally useful framework from which revisions can be made.

Figure 5.2. Maternal and Child Health Program Priorities

---

First-Order Priorities:   Survival
     Nutrition
     Health education
     Child spacing
     Environmental sanitation and water supply
     Day care for industrial centers

Second-Order Priorities:   Health Maintenance
     Shelter and housing
     Immunization
     Trained midwifery services
     Screening procedures
     Primary care clinics (health centers)

Third-Order Priorities: Improved Quality of Living
     Diagnostic and treatment referral centers
     School health programs
     Day care centers
     Homemaker and home health care services
     Foster home services

Fourth-Order Priorities:   Special Services
     Special services and education for the blind, deaf,
        handicapped, premature infants, etc.

Fifth-Order Priorities:   Complete Gradient of
                          Services

---

Source:   B. A. Miller and R. W. Noyes, "Priorities in Maternal and Child Health," in Community Medicine in Developing Countries, ed. A. R. Omran (New York: Springer, 1984).

Survival issues generally include nutrition, health education, child spacing, environmental sanitation, water supply, and day care for industrial centers. We have discussed some of these, but I want to go back and speak further about them. Health education may not be the term that most fully describes working with community groups to influence their own survival. Steuart's presentation appropriately placed health education in the context of facilitating constructive community organization. Instruction is also appropriate on such issues as breastfeeding and child safety.

Day care for industrial centers was an item that was debated long and hard before adding it to the survival group of issues. Its appropriateness was emphasized by Moser's report on the toddler who fell off the walk into the water. With the migration of people to industrial centers and the loss of traditional extended

family supports, some special provision for care of
infants and small children in order to ensure their survival that is not necessary in other parts of a country.
The scheme as developed presented shelter and
housing for most people as a health maintenance issue
but not a survival issue. A decade ago another conference in this country (Los Angeles, 1972, AMA sponsorship) reviewed the epidemiological evidence available
at that time linking health with habitat. The proven
linkages, particularly for such issues as overcrowding,
were less firm than conventional wisdom suggested. Referring to the trinity in Figure 5.1, John Cassell,
suggested a reason why research findings do not link
housing and health more dramatically. Strong social
support systems mitigate the adverse effects of poor
housing for many people, at least in relation to basic
survival issues. Maintaining good health over an extended period or improving the quality of life raise
concern about housing to a higher level of relevance.
    The scheme of priorities may provide clues to a
number of researchable questions, but to formulate and
answer them something more is needed. Research on health
requires use of some measurable markers or indicators of
acceptable levels of health. When defining health in
terms of adaptation, the available markers take the form
of measurements of maladaptation.
    Interest in such measurements in this country has
been stimulated by national policy changes since 1981.
Those policy changes diminished support for resources
and for services, especially for poor people. Proponents of the changes held that reductions involved only
wasteful expenditures. Policy analysts were faced with
the need to evaluate the new policies by measuring their
impact on the health of vulnerable populations. What
measurements could be used? The answer to that question
is useful for evaluating policies, whether the policy
concerns the reduction of a health services budget or
the improvement of housing.
    The measurements of greatest interest are termed
health outcomes. They are the health status measures,
expressed usually in negative terms of maladaptation. A
few service or process measures that enjoy proven
records for risk reduction are also appropriately
considered. For example, measurements on the proportion
of sexually active populations making use of
contraception (a process) are more useful than attempts
to measure the proportion of pregnancies that are
unwanted (an outcome). Such process measures, or
proxies for health outcomes, also include rates of
immunization and prenatal care.
    Most health outcome measures are rates based on a
known population base. Infant mortality or immunization
rates are the best known examples. A different approach
identifies a group of health outcomes that are useful

even without knowing the population base. Examples in
an industrial nation would be a case of diphtheria, or a
maternal death from septic abortion. Those outcomes,
termed "sentinel events,"[3] should simply never happen.
Even one case without respect to the population base
serves as an indicator that careful community diagnosis
and corrective action are required to prevent similar
outcomes among other people who may share risk of the
event. In Moser's discussion of the Guayaquil shantytown, the death of a child by fall from a walkway is a
sentinel event of importance even without knowing how
many other children have shared that same fate or how
many others are at risk of it. Data gathering on the
latter issues may be useful for establishing priorities
or for achieving political action, but even one event is
sufficient to indicate that a problem exists.

The first part of figure 5.3 presents a list of
health outcomes that were developed for use in monitoring and evaluating health policies in this country.
The list was compiled according to simple criteria: (a)
available data; (b) a panel of experts agreed on their
significance as measures or indicators of health; (c)
experience was sufficient to assure that the conditions
could be influenced by known interventions.

I should emphasize that the health outcome measures
serve a twofold purpose: they have value in their own
right, but they serve to improve understanding of broader issues that are more difficult to measure. Infant
mortality is a good example. Saving babies is a social
value that doesn't need defense in many modern cultures.
The cause has merit of its own. Beyond that value, the
measure aids understanding of a cluster of related issues, including nutrition, habitation, prenatal care,
and the role of women. Those values are difficult to
measure directly. The point becomes important when evaluating alternative policies that are linked to the
measures. For example, major medical centers can dramatically influence the infant mortality rate by saving a
few very low birth weight babies, flying them at high
cost by helicopter to intensive care units. The value
that cherishes babies has been protected and the
statistics have improved, but the significance of those
statistics as surrogate measures for quality of life
issues has been lost because we no longer focus on the
society as a whole and the well being of the greatest
number.

FIGURE 5.3. Proposed U.S. Child Health Outcome
Indicators and Sentinel Events

---

Infant mortality rate
Low birth weight rate
*Inadequate prenatal care
Congenital rubella syndrome
Congenital syphilis
Mental retardation associated with PKU or
    hypothyroidism
*Inadequate immunization rate
Measles--cases and deaths
Tetanus--cases and deaths
Diphtheria--cases and deaths
Vitamin D deficiency rickets--cases
Population-based growth stunting
Iron deficiency anemia
Infantile diarrhea--deaths
Elevated blood lead levels
Appendicitis--deaths
Motor vehicle accident fatalities
Nonmotor vehicle accident fatalities
Child abuse or neglect
Suicide

### Additional Indicators, Especially For Third World Nations

*Unattended childbearing
Maternal mortality rate
Post-neonatal mortality rates
Population growth
Birth rates
Family size
Kwashiorkor and nutritional marasmus
Other infection rates
Tuberculosis
Malaria
Whooping cough
Childhood deaths from pneumonia
Childhood deaths from burns
*Universal participation in some defined cluster of
    essential services

*Process measures of universally accepted value

---

Source:  L. B. Schorr, C. A. Miller, and A. Fine, "Over-
view and Context of Current Monitoring Efforts Using
Child Health Outcome Measures," in Monitoring Child
Health in the U.S.:  Selected Issues and Policies, ed.
D. K. Walker and J. B. Richmond (Cambridge, MA:  Harvard
University Press, 1983), pp. 7-33.

A few of the proposed outcome measures that did not make the final list may be of interest. Days lost from school is an example. That measure was discarded as an indicator of health: for many populations staying away from school to attend to other pressing matters (infant or sickness care, income supplementation) may represent a higher level of function than attending school.

The list of outcome measures is not proposed for use everywhere. It was designed for the United States, where we have substantial populations with problems not unlike those in some Third World countries. Even in the United States, the measures would be used selectively according to different circumstances, priorities, and community interests. Some measures lend themselves to different size populations and to different time spans. For example, infant mortality rates require a very large population and are not very useful with small groups over short periods. On the other hand, the proportion of pregnant women participating in early and continuous prenatal care is a useful indicator that is closely related to infant mortality. The data can be meaningfully gathered over short periods of time and for relatively small populations.

The list would require substantial revision to make it appropriate for Third World countries. Some possible appropriate health indicators are listed at the bottom of Figure 5.3.

One of the suggested measures for which there is increasing interest is the universal participation of a given population in some defined cluster of essential services, no matter how meager those services might be. A lesson can be learned from places like Sri Lanka and Kerala. Those states have resources that are as meager as any place in the world, with per capita annual income rates that are extremely low. Yet they have achieved health outcomes in terms of infant mortality rates and life expectancy that are exceedingly impressive. Sri Lanka has an infant mortality rate that is substantially better than that of our own capital city, Washington, D.C. In that city, we have sophisticated, elaborate technological services that are sometimes available to some people. There is no consistent effort to assure that the entire population is involved in early and continuous prenatal care, nutrition supplementation, immunization, or in any other cluster of services that can be defined. Sri Lanka, on the other hand, assures that all appropriate people participate in programs of nutrition, education, and family planning and attempts to upgrade those services over time. The benefits of near-universal participation in services reach far beyond what can be explained by the content of the services themselves. I have to believe that one of the benefits is promotion of a sense that health is an important _social_ value.  It may therefore become easier for people to adopt health-promoting behaviors as an important _personal_ value.  In the last analysis, personal behavior patterns continue to have the most profound influence on health outcomes.  The promotion of healthful personal behavior becomes exceedingly difficult in a society that collectively neglects people.

This view suggests that a useful organizing principle of health policy may be the selection of achievable and well-identified health outcomes for entire populations and wide promotion of the antecedent resources and services that show best promise for achieving those outcomes.  This approach contradicts extensive experience with demonstration projects that sought to saturate a small portion of a population with all defensible supports and services.  Those demonstrations are costly.  Ordinarily they are successful, except for one great failing--they seldom are extended to reach everyone who would benefit from similar interventions.

As a basis for developing a research agenda, the following scheme may be useful.  It attempts to rationalize the development of health supports and services, whether they be improved housing or better personal health services.  The scheme is as follows:

(a)  Definition of data and the sources for measuring health status (largely outcomes), risks, and trends.  Data must be available in a timely fashion and must be designed for populations of various sizes.  Data systems should be understandable to natural leaders among the affected population.

(b)  Monitoring systems, including sample survey techniques, must be developed to evaluate changes in population and in the physical and social environments.

(c)  Health status and risk measures should form the basis for defining specific, quantified health objectives.  The affected community should participate in selecting these measures and in establishing their significance as objectives.

(d)  Judgment must be exercised, making use of whatever research findings are available, in identifying the resources and processes that are appropriate for achieving the objectives.

The research agenda on habitation and health seeks better information on these issues, especially on the chain that links resources, interventions, and specific health outcomes.  This approach seeks to spare communities and nations the expense of allocating resources that meet the needs of some special provider system, but not the health needs of communities.

My formulation emphasizes data systems and measurement.  I defend that emphasis as the essential basis for research.  Important as measurement may be, it is not necessarily sufficient for effective public policy regarding housing, health, or any other cause. Policies and governments come and go, and their movements have little to do with better data. Ideologies and value systems are involved. Some of the values that we hold dearest are not readily measured, and they appropriately form the basis for much effective public policy. But on the other hand, policies are not apt to endure in the long run if they are not consistent with available evidence of effectiveness. I do not hold that social action for health or for housing should be delayed while the epidemiologists refine their tools. We must, however, help the epidemiologists understand which salient health issues are waiting to be clarified.

## NOTES

[1]Caroline O. N. Moser, "A Home of One's Own: Squatter Housing Strategies in Guayaquil, Ecuador," in Urbanization in Contemporary Latin America, ed. Alan Gilber, Jorge E. Hardoy, and Ronaldo Ramirez (New York: John Wiley and Sons, 1982).

[2]The Pruitt-Igoe project, built in St. Louis in 1954, became a symbol of the worst in ghetto living. After many costly efforts to reform and salvage it, it was dynamited and leveled. See Lee Rainwater, "The Lessons of Pruitt-Igoe," The Public Interest, 6-9 (1967).

[3]This is a term coined by Rutstein in D. D. Rutstein, W. Berenberg, T. C. Chalmers, C. G. Child, A. P. Fishman, and E. B. Perrin, "Measuring the Quality of Medical Care: A Clinical Method," New England Journal of Medicine 294 (1976):582-588.

# Discussion

Alonso:   The purpose of this meeting is not to deal,
once again, with the nature of underdevelopment or the
urban problem.   There have been many such meetings, and
there's no comparative advantage to dealing with those
issues here.   The reason I came was that the proper
agenda of the meeting is more narrow, and in a sense
more challenging, that is, to discover what the two pro-
fessions   or   disciplines--health   and   settlement/urban
habitat/shelter--might do better if they acted together.
The joint action of both viewpoints might be more powerful than separate viewpoints in dealing with some of
these issues.
   Most traditional urban planning, of course, for the
last couple of millennia, anyway, has derived from concerns about health.   Surely in modern times the adaptation to the urban explosion of Europe and the United
States in the nineteenth century is full of it, from the
development of engineering to sewers, and the various
health-based movements such as parks and housing reform.
The association of urban planning and housing is a very
traditional one.   It dates back to the Renaissance, to
medieval times, to Rome.
   It seems to me that we have not yet formulated  the
relationship between health and settlement in a really
fruitful way.   What I'm searching for is what Robert
Myerson first called a middle-range theory or a middle-
range theory break.   Something that is not so general
that you can't do anything about it, or so picky that it
makes  no  difference,  but  something  that's  about  the
right level.
   For instance, students, professionals, or agencies
have an initial interest in housing because they wish

97

well for their fellow human beings. In an area where
many people are ill-served, they want to do something.
Getting into it, they learn a bit more, and then realize
that inadequate housing is an expression of underlying
poverty. The problem is not housing per se--the problem
is poverty. Then they move onto social policy, not just
housing policy, when dealing with poverty. Then they say
poverty is not just circumstance, it's an expression of
the system. Now we must change the system. This kind of
intellectual migration from a particular agenda to a
much more general one is  frequent.

Let me give an analogous example from the settlement literature.  First the interest is in settlement
patterns, either from geography or from a policy point
of view. Then comes the recognition that the settlement
pattern is not like a furniture arrangement, but is an
expression of the spatial division of labor. This is
followed by the recognition that spatial division is an
expression of the social economy, and then, in many
cases, the recognition that it is an expression of the
international division of labor in the world economic
order.

In my more recent contacts with the health field,
I've noticed a similar phenomenon:  many of the traditional interests have been medical and biological.  Now
there is a recurring theme that this is not enough, that
one must understand the situation, the ecology, the
social values, and so on.

I would like to suggest that sometimes it makes
sense to try the opposite strategy:  that is, to look
for issues where health and settlements can go their own
separate ways.  For instance, I think some urban problems are problems in cities, not problems of cities. I
think that racial problems in the United States are
problems in cities, not problems of cities, as such. I
suspect certain forms of malnutrition, similarly, may
occur because people are in cities, not because of the
cities, in this sense.

From a slightly different angle, both the settlement people and the health people seem to be well-
intentioned and wish well for people.  Basically we want
people to lead good lives in humane societies.  But what
is the consequence of saying that the housing problem
cannot be solved and the nutrition problem cannot be
solved until the fundamental socioeconomics are tackled?
Why don't you say, "The hell with the housing problem
and its politics. I'm going up to the Sierras"?  Who is
to do housing or nutrition in the meantime?

Let me try to come down a little bit from the level
of abstraction and do it by reference to Jorge Enrique
Hardoy's work, particularly the case where he considers
the house and its immediate surroundings. What does
putting in water latrines or tiles do for what particular disease?  If you are handling resources, would you

insist on certain things and not others? What kind of information about the etiology of these diseases, about their functioning, will you need to know to make decisions on matters of housing design and the like? What are the main decisions? For instance, Jorge Enrique gives an example of water closets, and among the things he thinks this might affect would be schistosomiasis, partly by breaking the cycle and by disposing of human feces away from a source accessible to the snails. It occurs to me that this is a very possible thing to do. In some cases, you might find that in certain portions of the world there are other animal species that are also host to the parasite. In those situations, you would not deplete the parasite in the snail population simply by eliminating the cycle in human feces. In other cases, you might. What I'm saying is that here is a question where one might be able to find out and therefore make an intelligent decision. I think there is a failure of professional practice in establishing norms and strategies to inspect these realities, and I suggest that we could do a lot better in our concrete actions and recommendations.

Other issues come to mind. For instance, in the planning stage of irrigation projects, there will be economic analysis, there will certainly be engineering analysis, but very seldom will there be an analysis of the change in disease regime that will come about with a change in water regime. Thus, for instance, you dam the Volta and you go from the river blindness of moving water to schistosomiasis. This seems to come as a surprise, but it comes as a surprise every time. Couldn't something be done to anticipate these related changes?

We know that in the area of health, the research centers in the last century have been in the rich countries, for all of the obvious reasons. They are still in the rich countries, and the research agenda in medical biology and related areas has been the diseases of the rich countries, with a minor and often colonial orientation to the diseases in the hot countries. A classic example is the Panama Canal and yellow fever. The research that goes into warm-climate health problems is relatively small and concentrated, both in its expenditures and in the research establishments, in the rich countries. The bulk of the research will probably continue to be laboratory research and some of these serious problems, if they're solved, may well be solved by the laboratory approach rather than through the health settlement/ecology types of approaches.

However, I have come, in the past few years, to a much greater appreciation than I used to have of one particular problem. In these underdeveloped countries, half the population is kids. Because of differential fertility, there are more poor kids than poor adults, so the problem of poverty is really a problem of kids. The

question of kids is a question of family, a question of
women, a question of education, a question of nutrition,
fecundity, general health, mortality, family planning,
women's organizations, and so on.

What relations are going to emerge from any effort
that develops between the organizations and the people
of the poor countries to which these issues are addressed? Again, my advice is that we be very bloody-
minded about particular problems, the problems that
we're all trying to get past a little bit. If we tri-
vialize it and say, "Well, now, we'll just put one from
health, and one from settlements, and that'll do the
collaboration," we'll screw it up for sure. Another
problem is that, in research, funding, or similar areas,
the large bureaucracies must sign agreements and papers
and so forth. That presents a problem in reaching the
informal sector that many of us think must be reached.

Fisher: It is important to focus on our themes,
what we are going to talk about and what we can't talk
about. In dealing with health or urban and regional
planning programs in developing countries, it's also
important for us to keep repeating to ourselves and
others the significance of those programs, organizations, or efforts at identifying objectives. It's not
always appropriate to expect a final decision on what a
program's objective ought to be at any one time. In my
limited experience, social programs, including health
programs, have failed when their objectives were not
identified. Nobody really knew what the organization
existed for, or it was clear at an earlier time and is
forgotten today. For those programs that involve community organization, I think the point is well-made. Community organizations tend to work when they have a purpose, and when that purpose can be met--when there can
be some success in a finite period of time with a
practical amount of effort. When that's not clear, when
the organizations can't achieve or keep achieving
identifiable objectives, they disappear, fail, and are
in some senses counterproductive.

The point's been made again about the importance of
having a comprehensive view of things, of realizing that
there are many necessary conditions to making progress
in the achievement of health or any other objectives.
You've got to have the long-run model in sight, but in
fact there's no one cataclysmic or revolutionary step to
take that gets to the final result very fast--not
always, at least, not as often as we'd like. I think the
practical examples of that statement abound in the
success stories we have had. One of the great successes
in irrigated agriculture is what's called the training
and visitation system, in which the extension workers
engage in a program of training, have specific agricultural messages explained to them every two to three
weeks, and some kind of a small training center operated

by agricultural professionals is provided. Then the farmers, or the lead farmers, are visited with a specific
message, with a specific agricultural package or bit of
advice on what to do at a particular time of year with a
particular crop in particular soil. The system was
wildly successful, at least for a lot of irrigated agriculture. But the same sort of thing seems to be echoed
in what I'm hearing here, that if the health worker, the
health program, the community organization has a clear
purpose that is feasible and good, and, furthermore, if
that message can change over time--if the particular
objective is met, or is discovered not to be feasible,
then something else can be substituted--then something
successful can occur. That seems to me a good thing.

On the issue of data, the question comes up, how
much data and information are needed to understand and
to make decisions? What we're really talking about here
is the importance of being clear about what we have to
know in order to make decisions. To know that, we have
to know what the standards are. Again, the more clear
and explicit we can be in deciding what those standards
ought to be, the easier it is to know what data we need.
Without those standards, research, data collection,
whatnot, can be a terribly expensive, useless, or often
counterproductive exercise.

The IRRI center for international research in rice
in the Philippines is a booming success. Why? Well, for
one, they have a very clear objective: increase rice
yields. Also, maybe it's a simpler problem than reducing fertility or dealing with nutrition. It was,
however, substantially international, it was funded in-
ternationally, it was set up in a kind of isolation from
the Philippines itself, even though that was the immediate subject. It had a very large international professional community to call on. There were people that
could look at the technical agronomy issues and work by
themselves. There were others--sociologists and eco-
logists--who could work on other things, but they could
do it without having to report to a government right
away. They were able to do it, they kept getting money
to do it, I think largely because they could demonstrate
success in achieving very explicit objectives. The green
revolution came about largely because of that research.
I don't know if that's possible in health fields, but if
it isn't possible, I don't have an answer to the
research problem.

Satterthwaite: I would love to think that everyone
went through the intellectual migration Alonso talked
about, from "the problem is housing," to "the problem is
poverty," to "the problem is poverty as the expression
of a system." But a lot of people are still thinking
that the problem is lack of knowledge among the poor and
cultural inhibitions that stop them from solving their
own problems, not "the problem is the wider system." I

think the example of IRRI is a pertinent one. Where are the highest rice yields in the world? Japan, South Korea, Taiwan, Republic of China. Is it information that's caused that, or is it a fundamental land reform, the removal of the most exploitative tenancy relationships? Why has the phenomenal growth of the pharmaceutical industry not actually solved a lot? Why has schistosomiasis not been solved with a vaccine? A lot of drug companies are making a fortune out of the chemical therapy for schistosomiasis that has to be administered every two or three months. If you can find an immunization technique against schistosomiasis, you lose an enormous market. Now again I'm exaggerating on the other side, but would you like to respond to that?

Alonso: I was using the example of the vaccine vs. an ecological approach as an example in which pure voluntarism won't do. I have some colleagues who argue that in agriculture, for instance, some of the real revolutionary increases in productivity have been in hybrids. The advantage of hybrids is that they can be commercialized--you must buy the seed--which is a similar observation to yours. I think, from what I can see, that there are people trying to find vaccines. I don't know if they will. My point was with the hypothetical case, that if the odds of success are equal for both approaches, it so happens that most of the push is going on in the labs.

Crumley: It's been a frustrating four days for the social scientists here because you are basically reinventing what we do, in the sense that some scientists have been committed for seventy-five years or so to figuring out how to find information, how to strike a balance between a quantitative and a qualitative approach, how to determine in whose vested interests all of those things are taking place, how to figure out not only the small-scale community approaches, but also the macroscales of relations in terms of international questions, particularly in medical sociology and medical anthropology. We have a graduate student in our department who is sitting in a hut somewhere in Kenya trying to figure out what the relationship is between animal feces and certain kinds of diseases that appear to be getting into the food supply in certain kinds of ways. She's standing around watching to see whether people wash their hands, use the same pots, or whatever.

Our field of study has always been both practical and theoretical, and those questions have come up again and again in the discussion. We're aware of having to step back and look at what we're trying to do and get down and get dirty and do it. I think we have taken up the question, particularly in sociology and medical anthropology, of how we go about finding out those sorts of things in order to give professionals in other fields recommendations, mainly in the two disciplines that you have mentioned, planning and health.

Exactly what is each of us doing here, and why are we so interested in this? As an anthropologist, I am hopelessly frustrated at the notion of changing anything in any culture. But as social scientists we have in common a much longer time frame than either people in planning or in health. We see change and variety in the things that have come and disappeared from the face of the earth in the last three million years in the way of human settlements, so that one has a sort of abstract "Well, it's going to happen anyway" approach. But I don't think that that necessarily requires us to abandon the humanism I think all of us feel, and it's simply a question of trying to balance out those two things. I do think that the major focus is to figure out how those two groups of scholars are going to interact.

Hardoy: I'd like to pick up one issue you mentioned, the problem of work safety. In recent years many countries have been trying to pass laws for work safety, and not only for work safety, for protection of the working environment. Strangely, interest in legislation on the working environment has not been paralleled by an interest in legislation on the living environment. I bring up this issue because many of these workers, who just by the fact that they work in an environment that is protected by legislation--we could call them "official workers"--are merged into the official system of labor of their particular country. The interesting fact is that most of these workers live in illegal environments. In the best of cases, these workers will receive from the factories where they work some sort of health assistance, even though much of this health service is just a control for absenteeism. It's mostly a statistical survey of how many workers claim to be sick and don't work, rather than an attempt to improve the health situation. Now this split between the official working place and the illegal living place in a way epitomizes the whole situation of which we have been speaking. On the one hand, you have governments operating in a city at many levels of decisionmaking, with many ministries involved. At the same time you have thousands of impulses that are individually organized, sometimes with family help assistance, sometimes with community assistance. These are parallel to the official effort, and these parallel activities are building the urban environment in the Third World today. They are creating types of habitats which we hardly understand. I expect that there is a similar parallelism between an official system of health and the impulses of people who are trying somehow to achieve better health to keep them going.

Much of the trouble we have in research on problems of the environment is that we tend to engage in horizontal research, something that reflects a situation in a specific time. We hardly know about the processes that are really involved in this relationship between official and nonofficial systems operating in the construction of the city and their relationship to the official and nonofficial systems of health provision, and so on. The hardest problem is to understand which are the entry points to the study of habitat and health unless we think in a dimension that allows us to understand something about processes. I remember one day about fifteen years ago, the head of the Ford Foundation in Latin America asked me, "George, to what sort of research would you give priority?" And I said, "It's a very inexpensive research. Let's select one city of say 20-50,000 thousand people and do research on key issues, and then let's follow this city for ten to fifteen years, and try to find out, truly, what is involved, how the municipal government operates, how the relationships between the municipal, provincial, and national government operate. This can also be duplicated for health, and for the national, provincial, local, and private levels of housing, shelter, and construction, and so on." I still keep on struggling in order to understand these things, not only in specific terms--for instance, the subject of norms in relation to building and health that Arden Miller mentioned--but in terms of time span and process.

Moser: Lisa Peatie, who I think is one of the most eminent anthropologists in America, made a statement in her last book: "I'm an anthropologist, but I joined the planners a long time ago." In this book, she describes what it's like working at MIT as an anthropologist with a planner for twenty years. I take a less cynical, less depressing view of the capacity for interdisciplinary cooperation than other people, maybe because I've never worked in an academic department myself, and therefore my perception is different. I think that the critical thing is the recognition that we are moving from a concern with individual disciplines to a concern with areas.

# CHAPTER 6

# Water Supply and Health in Developing Countries: Selective Primary Health Care Revisited

JOHN BRISCOE

In the health delivery systems of most developing countries, the bulk of available resources is devoted to curative services delivered from urban hospitals.[1] With the exception of a few vertical programs, such as smallpox and yaws programs, health services have remained largely curative and largely unavailable to poor urban and especially rural people.[2] There have been, however, some dramatic exceptions to this general pattern. Of particular importance is the health care delivery system developed in the world's most populous country, the People's Republic of China,[3] but equally striking successes have been achieved in Sri Lanka, Kerala, Vietnam, and Cuba.[4]

In light of the failure of most countries to deliver health services to the majority of their people, and the success of other countries with similar resource bases in reaching this goal, WHO, UNICEF, and other international agencies embarked on an ambitious effort to encourage more countries to adopt the principles that had proved so successful in the abovementioned countries.

At the Alma Ata Conference in 1978, the characteristics of the successful systems were analyzed and the concept of primary health care (PHC) was defined and endorsed by all participating countries. Of particular importance in this definition is the explicit recognition given to the multiple causes of poverty and the manifestation of these causes in ill health. The strategy for dealing with health care issues was defined as

a multifactorial approach rather than simply a set of
medical activities. In particular, PHC was to include:

> education concerning prevailing health prob-
> lems and the methods for preventing and con-
> trolling them; promotion of food supply and
> proper nutrition; an adequate supply of safe
> water and basic sanitation; maternal and child
> health care, including family planning; immu-
> nization against the major infectious dis-
> eases; prevention and control of locally en-
> demic diseases; appropriate treatment of com-
> mon diseases and injuries; and provision of
> essential drugs.[5]

Shortly after Alma Ata, two biomedical scientists,
Walsh and Warren, published a critique of this PHC concept in the New England Journal of Medicine.[6] This critique and the alternative selective primary health care
(SPHC) concept advocated by Walsh and Warren have received widespread and generally favorable attention in
the scientific and development communities.

The reasoning behind the concept of SPHC is simple.
While the adherents to the idea profess sympathy with
the concept of comprehensive PHC as expressed in the
Alma Ata Declaration, they are acutely aware of the limited resources available to developing countries for
implementing PHC programs and argue that insufficient
resources are available to implement all components of
the original PHC program. What is necessary, then, is to
examine each possible item in the overall program individually, determine what the costs of implementing that
item are, and what the effectiveness of the program is
in reaching any particular objective. The items are then
ranked in terms of cost-effectiveness, and the SPHC program is designed to include the most cost-effective
items within the overall budgetary constraints per-
taining in any particular circumstance. The approach is
thus presented as simply a minor modification of the
original concept expressed in the Alma Ata Declaration,
a modification that adheres to the principles of Alma
Ata but makes the concept of PHC operational and imple-
mentable.

The SPHC package emerging from the cost-effectiveness calculations is almost exclusively medical--
including measles and diphtheria-pertussis-tetanus vac-
cinations; treatment for febrile malaria; oral rehydration for diarrhea in children; and tetanus toxoid for
mothers. Biomedical research for the development of
vaccines and therapies for major tropical diseases, too,
are considered "cost-effective." More systemic nonmedical activities such as community water supply, sanitation, and nutrition supplementation are rejected as
being "non-cost-effective."

The rationale of the SPHC approach has been widely accepted by both the scientific community (a computer search turned up dozens of references to the original article, with virtually all the articles accepting the premises of the SPHC approach in toto) and by policymakers in many international agencies. The recent U. S. Agency for International Development (AID) health sector policy is an outstanding example of the application of these principles.[7] This chapter examines the details of the cost-effectiveness calculations with respect to one of the components of PHC (community water supply), the choice of measures of effectiveness and the methodology used in comparing activities that fulfill different objectives. The rationale behind SPHC is also examined as it sheds light on the experience of both successful and unsuccessful national and pilot projects. The chapter concludes with a consideration of the programmatic and political consequences of SPHC vis-à-vis PHC.

## WATER SUPPLY AND SANITATION COST-EFFECTIVENESS

A computer search was carried out to identify articles in the scientific literature that referred to the original Walsh and Warren article. Many of these only reinforced the contention that a particular field of inquiry was important, but some of the articles presented a criticism of some details of the cost-effectiveness calculations. In this spirit, a critique of the numbers used by Walsh and Warren in assessing the cost-effectiveness of investments in water supply and sanitation is presented here.

The data used by Walsh and Warren for the capital costs of water supply and sanitation programs are based on recent and widely verified World Bank data, and aside from noting that in certain circumstances (such as tubewells in rural Bangladesh[8] and latrines in Zimbabwe[9]) the per capita costs may be an order of magnitude less than the costs used by Walsh and Warren, there is no basis for disagreement with the cost data used. Walsh and Warren do not appreciate, however, that whether or not there are additional investments in water supplies, people in many Third World settings (particularly in urban areas) pay substantial amounts of money for poor quality water supplies. A well-documented, but by no means unique, case is that of poor people in Lima, Peru[10], the results of which are summarized in Table 6.1 below.

TABLE 6.1. Water Use and Expenditures in Lima, Peru

| Quality of Service | Quantities Used (1/cap/day) | Monthly Household Expenditures on Water (soles) |
|---|---|---|
| Poor (vendors) | 23 | 105 |
| Medium (standpipe) | 78 | 22 |
| Good (house connection) | 152 | 35 |

Table 6.1 shows that improvements in the quality of water supply service in urban areas may be associated not with an <u>increase</u> but with a <u>reduction</u> in the monetary costs of the supply, a finding by no means unique to Lima. One of the most experienced water supply engineers in the world has found this phenomenon to be virtually universal in developing countries and has concluded that "if daily expenditures made to a water carrier were invested instead in a proper piped supply, far more economical and better water service could be provided."[11]

In terms of a cost-effectiveness analysis of the sort used by Walsh and Warren, then, the economic costs of such water supply improvements may be much smaller than the overall cost of the project, since much, or often all, of the costs can be covered by "simply" redirecting expenditures that are already being made by the population for an inferior water supply service. Since the Third World is rapidly becoming as much an urban as a rural world, since similar willingness to pay is often demonstrated by rural inhabitants[12], and since those urban dwellers paying high costs for poor water supplies also have the highest incidences of disease, this phenomenon is of major importance in terms of improving health through the investment of relatively few outside resources. The rub, of course, is in the word "simple," for these poor urban residents are frequently not recognized as either legitimate or deserving by their governments. The organizational and managerial implications of these changes are by no means trivial. A key issue, then, is political will and program management, themes to which this critique will return.

Turning to the denominator in the cost-effectiveness factor, an assessment of the likely impact of water supply and sanitation programs on health is far more problematic than an assessment of the effects of other PHC programs that operate more directly on the causes of disease. Thus, while it is a relatively straightforward (although not minor) task to calculate the effects of a tetanus or measles vaccine on death rates, a similar assessment of the effects of a water supply and sanitation program is fraught with problems, for the intervening steps linking the program inputs to health outputs are far more numerous and the necessary behavioral changes far more complex. In particular, the assumption that the water supply produces the quantity and quality of water for which it was designed is frequently incorrect, as is the assumption that the water supply is being used appropriately by the classes or age groups most affected by water-related diseases.[13]

In light of these problems, it is appropriate to proceed with caution in attempting to assign a "typical value" to the effect of water supply and sanitation programs on health.[14] In their analysis, Walsh and Warren used only a small sample of a large number of available studies and drew universal conclusions that are not supported by a more comprehensive assessment. For instance, Walsh and Warren concluded that while water piped into the home might result in substantial reductions in diarrheal diseases, water supplied through public standpipes would effect only a very small reduction (about 5 percent) in the incidence of diarrheal diseases. While this was certainly the conclusion to be drawn from the studies examined by Walsh and Warren, fundamental doubts have been raised about the results of one of the studies.[15] A more complete analysis of methodologically sound available studies would have indicated that where greater quantities of water of improved quality became available through standpipes, the expected reductions in diarrheal diseases were of an order of magnitude greater than the 5 percent assumed by Walsh and Warren. This is indicated on Table 6.2, which is abstracted from a recent comprehensive review of the health effects of water supply and sanitation programs.[16]

TABLE 6.2: Water Supply and Sanitation Programs in Twenty-four Nonintervention Studies

| Parameter Affected | Number of Studies | Reduction in % Diarrheal Diseases (Median) |
|---|---|---|
| Water quality | 6 | 30 |
| Water availability (mostly through standpipes) | 11 | 34 |
| Quality and availability | 4 | 40 |
| Excreta disposal | 8 | 40 |

There are reasons, then, to believe that the figures used by Walsh and Warren in both the denominator and numerator of the cost-effectiveness calculations for water supply and sanitation programs are in error. Furthermore, since the approach taken by Walsh and Warren is one in which the cost-effectiveness of different components of PHC is compared, it is pertinent to note that there are also serious problems with the costs and effectivenesses used by Walsh and Warren for the more traditional medical components. Their analysis suggested these measures were most appropriate in a "selective" approach. Specifically, in the examination of several small nongovernmental health projects[17] that served as a basic source of data for the Walsh and Warren analysis, "costs generally did not include capital investment, training, expenditures beyond the primary level of health care, or the value of expatriate and volunteer labor."[18] In scaling up these projects to a national level, the costs would be substantially greater and the effectiveness of the programs substantially less due to "political and administrative problems."[19] Indeed, making generalizations from these findings has been questioned by many (including the Director General of the WHO).[20] Typical of comments disputing generalizations were the remarks on the Indian project: "It was the dedication of the team leaders, their total involvement in the community programs, and their special organizational abilities which made the program successful."[21]

However, the SPHC analysis of Walsh and Warren is, in our opinion, flawed by conceptual problems that are more serious than the problems of detail outlined above. For this reason, it is not appropriate to present revised cost-effectiveness figures for water supply and sanitation programs and other components or to suggest, on the basis of such revised estimates, an alternative hierarchy of programs for SPHC.

## CRITERIA FOR ASSESSING THE EFFECTIVENESS OF HEALTH PROGRAMS

Health is a multifaceted concept. At the most elementary level, it is possible to distinguish between severity of effect (infection, disease, disability, and death), and age group affected (infant, child, or adult). A fundamental difficulty in comparing different health programs is that different programs usually affect different facets of health. One program, for instance, may affect infant mortality only, while another might affect infection, disease, disability, and mortality in all age groups.

It is immediately apparent, then, that in attempting to compare different health programs two questions are of fundamental importance: (a) what are the health outcomes that will be considered; and (b) who will judge the trade-offs between these outcomes? A first concern with the procedure followed by Walsh and Warren is their choice of criteria and the consistency (or lack thereof) in applying them to the components of PHC that they analyze. For the most part, Walsh and Warren consider reduction in infant mortality to be the unique criterion of interest, thus comparing, for instance, the cost per infant death averted through water supply and sanitation programs, expanded immunization, and oral rehydration therapy programs. This puts them in a bind, for such a procedure means that all programs that do not result primarily in reductions in infant mortality (one of those considered by Walsh and Warren is an onchocerciasis control program) will automatically be rejected. The procedure followed by Walsh and Warren, then, indicates that onchocerciasis control programs "prevent few infant deaths," leaving the reader to assume that onchocerciasis control programs should be rejected because they don't lead to reduction in infant deaths or only may be justified on grounds other than reductions in infant deaths.

With respect to the example that is followed through the present analysis--water supply and sanitation--Walsh and Warren follow a quite different procedure. Since it is never argued that the only effect of a water supply and sanitation program is a reduction in infant mortality, the only consistent procedure would be to repeat the procedure followed in the onchocerciasis control program and make no comparison between a water supply/sanitation program and a program whose effect is the reduction of infant mortality. This Walsh and Warren do not do. Instead, they compare water supply and sanitation programs with programs aimed specifically at reducing infant mortality (such as oral rehydration therapy programs) and conclude, not surprisingly, that programs that affect infant mortality only are more effective in this regard than programs with multiple effects. Walsh and Warren's procedure is equivalent to claiming that program B is superior to program C simply because B gives us more of outcome 1 than C (ignoring the fact that C gives us more of desirable outcome 2 than B).

As indicated earlier, trade-offs between different outcomes cannot be considered in isolation from the decision as to who will make such trade-offs. While Walsh and Warren could almost certainly defend their choice of reduction in infant mortality as an important criterion, other scientists would claim that different criteria (such as morbidity in the adult population) are important, too. Where different criteria are used, of course, the cost-effectiveness of different programs will vary accordingly. For example, in the case of cholera, rehydration therapy has been shown to be less costly and more effective in saving lives than immunization. When morbidity reduction becomes the objective, the results of the same cost-effectiveness analysis are reversed.[22]

In the spirit of John Grant, however, who argued that primary health care and other development programs should follow "the principle of inherent need and interest," in which "projects in a village should grow out of its own needs and interests, and not be superimposed by some idealists,"[23] we would argue that the trade-offs between the outputs of PHC programs be done in light of the expressed needs of the communities involved. From an examination of the actual health and nutrition practices of families in the developing world, it is clear that their de facto priorities do not agree with the assumption of Walsh and Warren that reductions in infant mortality are of singular concern. In particular, throughout the developing world, the economic welfare of families is highly dependent upon the economic production of adults.[24] This situation gives rise, for example, to discrimination in feeding among household members to protect the actual or potential breadwinner in subsistence settings.[25] In assessing actual practices, however, attention has to be given to the fact that families, like villages, are not division-free entities, and it is necessary to go one step further and ask whose interests in the family should be given greater weight.

From a variety of perspectives, it seems clear that those whose needs are most important in terms of the health of the community in general, and of young children in particular, are mothers. First, virtually all components of PHC programs are based on the assumption that mothers will be the most important front-line providers of health care to children.[26] Second, the most consistent correlate of infant health is the mother's education.[27] This implies that there are few better investments in health than those that meet the needs of women and, particularly, those that alleviate the limitations on the education of girls and women. Later it will be argued that a particularly important constraint faced by women in undertaking "discretionary activities"[28] such as education and child care is the enormous demand made on women to perform time-consuming, repetitive tasks. Investments that relieve mothers of a part of this burden will have an effect on child health that is as certain as it is impossible to quantify.[29] Indeed, many experienced investigators of the determinants of health in the Third World would concur with Latham, who has argued that "attentions to women's rights and the emancipation of women may ultimately have more impact on nutrition and infection in developing countries than any of the [conventional nutrition and health] interventions."[30]

Concurring, then, with the exhortation of the Director General of WHO that mothers become the subject and not the object of health programs, the following discussion assesses some principal constraints faced by women in implementing PHC programs.

## CONSTRAINTS ON WOMEN AS FRONT-LINE HEALTH CARE WORKERS

A concept central to all PHC programs is that no lasting advances in child health can be made unless the mother is involved in these programs. Thus, most of the core elements of PHC programs--such as breastfeeding, supplementary feeding, oral rehydration therapy, and household hygiene--involve the mother as the front-line health worker. Indeed, the objective of PHC programs may be described as the improvement of "mothering, the poorly-defined but crucial interactions between mother and child that form the principal determinants of health, growth and development."[31]

To carry out the complex and demanding task being set her by PHC programs, the mother faces four principal constraints: technology, knowledge, resources, and time. One way of visualizing PHC programs is as efforts to relieve the mother of one or more of these constraints so that she may become a more effective mother.

In their analysis of SPHC, Walsh and Warren focus their attention almost exclusively on the first of these four constraints, technology, an approach common to the policy formulations of some development agencies as well. While there is no doubt that technological advances, such as improved expanded vaccination programs and oral rehydration therapy, enlarge the potential for child health in developing countries, the provision of improved technology alone is insufficient. Usually the effective implementation of such technology requires simultaneous inputs of knowledge, resources, and time on the part of the mother. Let us consider a few examples.

### Breastfeeding

PHC programs provide information to the mother on the fundamental importance of breastfeeding for the health of her infant and technology in the form of programs designed to monitor the growth of her child. While such programs are essential, the mother must have time to breastfeed her baby. Studies throughout the world have shown that where women work outside the home, they do not have the time available to breastfeed their babies. Thus, the inputs of knowledge and technology provided by the PHC program cannot be translated into improved childrearing practices. (A finding in Malaysia is typical: women who were recently employed spent 33 percent less time breastfeeding their children than women in a control group who had not recently been employed.[32]

## Oral Rehydration Therapy (ORT)

Oral rehydration therapy (ORT) technology offers new opportunities for the reduction of mortality in young children in developing countries. As in all other cases, however, the provision of the technology alone will have little impact unless the constraints faced by the mother in using the technology are addressed simultaneously. The constraints are several: in many areas of the world, the cost of rehydration packages is too great for poor families.[33] In almost all situations, traditional understanding of food and liquid withdrawal during diarrhea must be changed.[34] Thus, the ORT technology has to be accompanied by education and information. Finally, since "continually giving a sick infant large volumes of liquid by spoon or cup is time-consuming, tiring, and inconvenient for an overburdened mother with other children plus household and farm work to do, ORT may require the commitment of more time and energy than she can easily provide."[35]

## Clinic-Based Supplementary Feeding and Other Programs

Perhaps the simplest of all programs, in principle, is one in which the mother comes to a clinic or distribution center to collect food for her child, to weigh her child, to have her child immunized. Yet many studies have shown that attendance at a clinic drops off dramatically as the distance to a clinic increases[36] and that women in the labor force are frequently unable to avail themselves of such programs because of the constraints on their time.[37]

## Food Preparation and Storage

Recent longitudinal studies in Bangladesh[38] and the Gambia[39] have documented the vital role of food contamination in the transmission of diarrheal diseases, an effect that becomes particularly marked when great demands are made on the time of the mother. In the Gambia, for instance, at the peak diarrheal transmission season, "feeding of small children is particularly haphazard. . . . Infants may be left in the compound in the care of young nursemaids with a supply of porridge or gruel for the next eight or nine hours, and food for the evening meal is sometimes stored overnight."[40]

In sum, the great demands placed on the time of Third World mothers constitute a serious barrier to the implementation of PHC. These constraints often are particularly acute at those times of the year when children have most need of additional health care[41] and in low-income families where the incidence of illness is greatest.[42] The overall effect of restrictions on the availability of time is evident in recent data from the Philippines. Although the children of working mothers received 5 percent more food than the children of a comparable group of mothers who were not working, the former weighed, on the average, 7 percent less than the latter, an effect attributed to the lack of time available to working mothers to translate increased resources and improved knowledge into improved health for their children.[43]

Thus, improved water supply and sanitation conditions affect PHC by reducing the disease load (see Table 6.2) and thus the need for child care; by increasing available income through reducing payments for water (see Table 6.1); and by releasing the calories used in carrying water (12 percent of a woman's caloric intake in East Africa).[44] However, the most important effect may be increasing the time available to mothers for carrying out child care and other "discretionary activities."

## MOTHERS' NEEDS IN DEVELOPING COUNTRIES

A recent workshop on "Women in Poverty" examined the phenomenon of poverty among women in the Third World and analyzed how women might become actors in and beneficiaries of the development process. Three conclusions of this workshop are of particular importance for PHC. First, time is the most important resource that poor women have available to them.[45] Second, studies in a variety of developing countries (Bangladesh, Bolivia, Indonesia, and the Philippines) have found that the rural mother engages in ten to eleven hours per day of active home and market production,[46] whereas women in industrialized countries typically work at and near the home only six hours per day.[47] Third, poverty is concentrated in female-headed households; the number of these households is large (usually between 15 percent and 35 percent) and increasing.[48] Thus, the workshop concluded that for women in developing countries "saving time is development, for time saved from humdrum tasks is time to invest in human capital" and that priority should be given to "technologies that reduce the time women and children spend fetching wood and water and preparing food."[49]

## TIME REQUIRED FOR WATER COLLECTION

The impact of the installation of a convenient village water supply system on the time spent by women and children in carrying water has been documented throughout the world.[50] To give just a few of many examples--

in the lowlands of Lesotho, 30 percent of families spend
over 160 minutes per day collecting water[51]; as a result
of improved water supplies in the Zaina scheme in Kenya,
about 100 minutes per household per day are saved from
the water-collecting activity.[52] In East Africa, rural
families spend up to 264 minutes per day carrying
water[53]; in East Nigeria, families spend up to 300
minutes per day collecting water.[54] Studies in Asia
(e.g., the Philippines[55] and Thailand[56]), also have
documented the substantial amount of time spent in
collecting water in many areas.

## NEEDS OF LOW-INCOME WOMEN

It would thus appear that a major constraint on women's
"discretionary activities" (including child care) in
many developing countries is the enormous demand made on
their time for the performance of repetitive, time-
consuming tasks. It has further been documented that in
many rural communities, the fetching and carrying of
water is one of the most important of these tedious
tasks. What do the low-income women of the Third World
have to say about this when they are asked directly,
when they are treated, as Halfdan Mahler would have it,
as subjects and not just as objects in the development
process?

In looking for answers to this question, it bears
repeating that societies in general, and societies in
developing countries in particular, are sharply divided
along class and sex lines. Earlier it was argued that
particular attention should be paid to the concerns of
poor women, yet determining the concerns of this largely
disenfranchised group is not simple for two reasons.
First, the sexual division of labor is universal. The
time-consuming tasks performed by women are seldom if
ever performed by men, and second, "the decisionmakers
or leaders in the agencies and in the target communities
are usually men and they communicate with other men and
not with the women."[57] Thus, as Elmendorf has documented for Kenya, the reduction in time-consuming tasks
like fetching and carrying water is a high-priority need
for rural women but is typically given low priority when
the "village leaders" (men) are asked for their opinion.

When surveys of community needs have taken account
of such factors throughout the developing world, water
supply has ranked high on the list of expressed priorities.[58] In a recent review of the findings of surveys
of low-income women in developing countries, water
supply improvements were found to "rank right alongside
the most basic human need [adequate food] in many [such]
surveys."[59]

## COST EFFECTIVENESS REVISITED

Returning to the decision model outlined earlier, it is apparent that when program outcomes are not restricted solely to reductions in infant mortality and, when the trade-offs between outcomes are made by poor Third World women and not scientists, water supply programs routinely constitute an integral part of PHC programs in those (large) areas of the developing world in which access to adequate water supplies is restricted.

It is not surprising that in all countries in which PHC has been successful, improvements in water supply and sanitation conditions have been an integral part of strategies for both improving health and improving the status of women.[60]

## SUMMARY AND CONCLUSIONS

Six years after Alma Ata, what is the prospect for the PHC philosophy as outlined in the Alma Ata Declaration? On the one hand, the concept is clearly a viable one that has been implemented successfully in a number of large, low-income developing countries and with considerable, if only temporary, success in a number of pilot projects in developing countries that have made little progress at the national level.[61] The overwhelming reality, however, is that in those countries that made little progress before Alma Ata, little progress in implementing PHC programs has been made since.[62] Simplifying a complex debate, there have been two contending explanations for this failure. Many have seen the failure of PHC programs in most developing countries as a predictable consequence of a "lack of political will." Others have focused on technical factors, such as the scarcity of resources for implementing PHC programs, and the necessity for making cost-effectiveness choices.

For those who favor the technical interpretation of this experience, the SPHC approach of Walsh and Warren is an insightful and pragmatic tool for making choices in the light of "resource scarcity" about which interventions are "cost effective." This analysis, however, is fundamentally flawed. If the problem is "resource scarcity," why have several low-income countries implemented strikingly successful PHC programs while many other countries with higher GNP per capita have failed completely? If the problem is the comprehensive nature of the Alma Ata formulation of PHC, then why have all the successful national programs taken such a comprehensive approach? If water supply and sanitation programs are not "cost effective," why is it that all the countries in which PHC has been effective made improvements in water supply and sanitation a cornerstone of their PHC approach? In summary, although the approach taken by Walsh and Warren and used as a basis for sector strategies by some international development agencies has a certain appeal to fundamental notions of rational planning, the approach fails to account for the experience that has occurred with PHC programs throughout the world. This being the case, then, there are several critical questions. Is there an alternative interpretation that explains the experience with PHC programs more satisfactorily? If so, what are the implications of this alternative interpretation for policy? Finally, why has the obviously flawed SPHC approach proved so compelling and attractive to some development agencies?

Even the technically focused analyses of the SPHC sort usually mention in passing the "importance of political will and management" in the implementation of PHC programs. An alternative explanation for the success of some national PHC programs and the failure of others considers this factor of political will to be fundamental rather than incidental. The importance of this commitment is evident from both longitudinal and cross-sectional observations. History shows that prior to World War II, cogent blueprints for appropriate health services were drawn up for China and India (in the form of the Bhore Commission Recommendations of 1943). To John Grant, who played a major role in this process in both countries and who recognized that "the use of medical knowledge . . . depends chiefly upon social organization,"[63] subsequent developments could have been no surprise. When the government made a fundamental commitment to meeting the health (and other) needs of all people, as in China, enormous progress was made in developing an appropriate health delivery system. When no such commitment was made, as in India, health services changed little over the intervening forty years.[64] Similarly, a contemporary cross-sectional comparison of countries that have made marked progress in the development of health services for the entire population with those countries that have developed adequate services for only a small minority shows that progress has been rapid only when "health and health care became a political goal and eventually came under political control as a part of overall development."[65]

To the proponents of this alternative interpretation, the experience of the successful nongovernmental PHC projects that are the object of so much attention in the cost-effectiveness analyses is consistent with this theory on the centrality of political commitment. What distinguishes these successful small projects from the unsuccessful national projects in the same countries is not available resources or technology. Through dedication and management these programs have managed to overcome the lack of political will that characterizes the national programs in these countries.[66]

Thus the concerns of the technical analysts with "resource constraints" and the use of "noncost-effective technologies" may not be entirely to the point. The problem of "resource scarcity" is a problem wrongly named. It arises not because there are insufficient resources for the health sector, but because the vast majority of these resources, both public and private, are devoted to an existing urban, hospital-based, capital-intensive health care system that is serviced by and meets the needs of an elite minority.[67] The problem of appropriate technology is a real one, and there is no doubt that, where political commitment exists, PHC programs will become more effective through the use of ORT, expanded immunization programs, improved low-cost sanitation technologies, and other technological improvements. This does not imply, however, that an enormous amount cannot be done with existing technologies. The successful experiences in China, Sri Lanka, Cuba, Vietnam, and Kerala all demonstrate the progress that can be made without the technological advances that some international development agencies consider the major impediment to improving health in developing countries. Indeed, the experience of successful national PHC programs shows that the issue of appropriate technology is intimately related to the issue of political commitment, as is evident in the development and widespread use of innovative "appropriate" solutions to the problems of sanitation technology in both China[68] and Vietnam[69] and the imaginative incorporation of traditional medicine into a modern health care delivery system in China.[70]

Given these manifest shortcomings of the Walsh and Warren type of approach, why has it proved so attractive to certain development agencies and many developing country governments? It helps deflect responsibility. The only reasonable conclusion from the evidence is that credit for the success, or blame for the failure, of national PHC programs lies squarely with the government of the country concerned. Where PHC programs have failed, it is because the commitment of the government to "health for all" its people is little more than empty rhetoric. The SPHC approach allows the lack of commitment to remain unidentified; thus, the government is free of any culpability.

The implication for development agencies with a genuine concern for the health of all people has been stated by one of the pioneers of the PHC movement: "Where support is available, let it be selectively directed to those countries which already have, or are taking steps to develop, a form of decision-making and implementation which is likely to be effective."[71] Since the support of some development agencies for certain countries has more to do with political imperatives than a true concern for the health of the

people of that country, these agencies use analyses such
as that presented by Walsh and Warren to deflect
responsibility for death and illness from its true
source, namely the home governments and their international supporters. They assign responsibility for such
suffering to "neutral" causes such as "resource shortages" and "the limitations of technology." In short,
selective primary health care is not, as the authors
would suggest, a practical modification of the PHC concept, but rather a negation of much that was positive in
the PHC approach formulated at Alma Ata.

## NOTES

[1]E. Stern, "Health and Development" (Paper presented at International Conference on Oral Rehydration
Therapy, Washington, D.C., June, 1983), passim.
[2]K. W. Newell, "Developing Countries," in Primary
Care, ed. J. Fry (London: Heinemann, 1980), pp. 196-218
[3]B. S. Hetzel, "Basic Health Care and the People,"
in Basic Health Care in Developing Countries: A
Epidemiological Perspective, ed. B. S. Hetzel (Oxford:
Oxford University Press, 1980), pp. 1-10.
[4]K. Djukanovic, "The Democratic Republic of North
Vietnam," in Basic Health Care in Developing Countries:
An Epidemiological Perspective, ed. B. S. Hetzel, (Ox-
ford: Oxford University Press, 1980) pp. 102-17, V. Na-
varro, "Health Services in Cuba: An Initial Appraisal,'
New England Journal of Medicine 287 (1972):954-959, K.
W. Newell, "Developing Countries," in Primary Care, ed.
J. Fry (London: Heinemann, 1980) pp. 196-218; J. Rat-
cliffe, "Social Justice and the Demographic Transition:
Lessons from India's Kerala State," International
Journal of Health Services 8 No. 1 (1978):123-44.
[5]World Health Organization, Declaration of Alma Ata
(Report on the International Conference on Primary
Health Care, Alma Ata, USSR, 6-12 September 1978),
passim.
[6]J. A. Walsh and K. S. Warren, "Selective Primary
Health Care: An Interim Strategy for Disease Control
in Developing Countries" New England Journal of Medicine
301(1979):967-974.
[7]United States Agency for International Development, AID Policy: Health Assistance (Washington, D.C.:
USAID, 1982a), passim.
[8]United States Agency for International Development, AID Policy Paper: Domestic Water and Sanitation
(Washington, D.C.: USAID, 1982b), passim.
[9]P. R. Morgan and D. D. Mara, Ventilated Improved
Pit Latrines: Recent Developments in Zimbabwe. World
Bank Technical Paper No. 3 (Washington, D.C.: World
Bank, 1982), passim.

[10]B. T. Adrianza and G. G. Graham, "The High Cost of Being Poor: Water," Archives of Environmental Health 28(1974):312-15.

[11]D. A. Okun, "Review of Drawers of Water," Economic Development and Cultural Change 23 No. 3(1975):580-583.

[12]United States Agency for International Development, The Potable Water Project in Rural Thailand, Washington, D.C.: USAID, 1980), passim.

[13]J. Briscoe, "The Role of Water Supply in Improving Health in Poor Countries (with Special Reference to Bangladesh)," American Journal of Clinical Nutrition, 31(1978):2100-2113.

[14]R. J. Saunders and J. J. Warford, Village Water Supply: Economics and Policy in the Developing World,. (Baltimore, MD: Johns Hopkins University Press, 1976), passim.

[15]D. Dworkin and J. Dworkin, "Water Supply and Diarrhea: Guatemala Revisited." AID Evaluation Special Study No. 2, (Washington, D.C.: USAID,1980), passim.

[16]J. M. Hughes, "Potential Impacts of Improved Water Supply and Excreta Disposal on Diarrheal Disease Morbidity: An Assessment Based on a Review of Published Studies," (Atlanta, GA: Center for Disease Control, 1983), passim.

[17]D. R.Gwatkin, J. R. Wilcox, and J. D. Wray, Can Health and Nutrition Interventions Make a Difference? (Washington, D.C.: Overseas Development Council, 1980), passim.

[18]J. R. Evans, K. L. Hall, and J. Warford, "Shattuck Lecture--Health Care in the Developing World: Problem of Scarcity and Choice," New England Journal of Medicine 305(1981):1117-1127.

[19]Evans, "Shattuck Lecture," passim.

[20]H. Mahler, "Preface," in D. R. Gwatkin et al., Can Health and Nutrition Interventions Make a Difference? (Washington, D.C.: Overseas Development Council, 1980), passim.

[21]R. Sharma and S. K. Chaturvedi, "India," in Hetzel, Basic Health Care, passim.

[22]L. C. Chen, "Control of Diarrheal Diseases Morbidity and Mortality: Some Strategic Issues," American Journal of Clinical Nutrition 31 No. 12(1978):2284-2291.

[23]J. B. Grant, Health Care for the Community, Selected Papers of Dr. John B. Grant, (Baltimore: Johns Hopkins University Press, 1963), passim.

[24]Chen, "Diarrheal Diseases," passim.

[25]D. Chernichovsky, "The Economic Theory of the Household and the Impact Measurement of Nutrition and Related Health Programs," Evaluating the Impact of Nutrition and Health Programs, ed. R. E. Klein (New Jersey: Plenum Press, 1979), passim.

[26]S. Cole-King, "Primary Health Care: A Look at Its Current Content," (New York: UNICEF, 1981), passim.

[27]W. H. Mosley, "Will Primary Health Care Reduce Infant and Child Mortality? A Critique of Some Current Strategies, with Special Reference to Africa and Asia" (Paper presented at IUSSP Seminar on Social Policy, Health Policy and Mortality Prospects, Paris, 1983), passim.

[28]J. P. Grant, "The State of the World's Children," 1983-83" (New York: UNICEF, 1982), passim.

[29]Saunders, Village Water, passim.

[30]M. C. Latham, in G. T. Keusch, "Resume of the Discussion on Interventions: Strategies for Success," American Journal of Clinical Nutrition 31 No. 12(1978):2352-2356.

[31]J. E. Rohde, "Preparing for the Next Round: Convalescent Care after Acute Infection," American Journal of Clinical Nutrition 31 No. 12(1978):2258-2268.

[32]N. Birdsall and W. P. Greevey, "The Second Sex in the Third World: Is Female Poverty a Development Issue?" (Paper summarizing findings of Workshop on Women in Poverty, International Center for Research on Women, Washington, D.C., 1978), passim.

[33]A. A. Kielmann and C. McCord, "Home Treatment of Childhood Diarrhea in Punjabi Villages," Journal of Tropical Pediatrics and Environmental Child Health 23 no. 4(1977):197:201.

[34]Academy for Educational Development, Results of Honduras Field Investigation (Washington, D.C.: AED, 1982), passim.

[35]R. L. Parker, W. Rinehart, P. T. Piotrow and L. Doucette, "Oral Rehydration Therapy for Childhood Diarreha." Population Reports L(2), 1980, passim.

[36]C. DeSweemer, in F. T. Koster, "Resume of the Discussion on Health Care Interventions." American Journal of Clinical Nutrition 31 no. 12(1978):2274-2278.

[37]B. M. Popkin and F. S. Solon, "Income, Time, the Working Mother and Child Nutriture," Journal of Tropical Pediatrics and Environmentsl Child Health (1976):156-66.

[38]R. E. Black, K. H. Brown, S. Becker, Arma Alim, and M. H. Merson, "Contamination of Weaning Foods and Transmission of Enterotoxiganic E. coli Diarrhea in Children in Rural Bangladesh." Transcripts of the Royal Children in Rural Bangladesh." Transcripts of the Royal Society of Tropical Medicine and Hygiene 76(1982):259-64.

[39]M. G. M. Rowland and J. P. K. McCollum, "Malnutrition and Gastroenteritis in the Gambia," Transcripts of the Royal Society of Tropical Medicine and Hygiene 71(1977):199-203.

[40]Roland, "Malnutrition," passim.

[41]L. C. Chen, A. K. A. Chowdhury, and S. C. Huffman, "Seasonal Dimensions of Energy Protein Malnutrition in Rural Bangladesh: The Role of Agriculture,

Dietary Practices, and Infection," Ecology of Food and Nutrition 8(1979):175-187.
    [42]B. M. Popkin, "Some Economic Aspects of Planning Health Interventions Among Malnourished Populations," American Journal of Clinical Nutrition 31 No. 12(1978): 2314-2323.
    [43]B. M. Popkin, "Time Allocation of the Mother and Child Nutrition," Ecology of Food and Nutrition 9(1980):1-14.
    [44]G. F. White, D. J. Bradley, and A. N. White, Drawers of Water Use in East Africa (Chicago: University of Chicago Press, 1972), passim.
    [45]Birdsall, "Second sex," passim.
    [46]Popkin, "Malnourished populations," passim.
    [47]Birdsall, "Second sex," passim.
    [48]Ibid.
    [49]Ibid, passim.
    [50]Saunders, Village Water, passim.
    [51]R. Feachem, E. Burns, S. Cairncross, A. Cronin, P. Cross, D. Curtis, M. K. Khan, D. Lamb, and H. Southall, Water Health and Development: An Interdisciplinary Evaluation (London: Tri-Med, 1978), passim.
    [52]I. D. Carruthers, Impact and Economics of Community Water Supply: A Study of Rural Water Investment in Kenya (London: Agrarian Development Unit, Wye College, 1973), passim.
    [53]White, Water Use, passim.
    [54]Feachem, "Water Health," passim.
    [55]Popkin, "Time allocation," passim.
    [56]USAID, Potable Water, passim.
    [57]M. Elmendorf, Women, Water and Waste: Beyond Access (Washington, D.C.: WASH Project, 1982), passim.
    [58]USAID, Potable Water, passim. A. N. White, "The Role of the Community in Water Supply and Sanitation Projects," in The Impact of Interventions in Water Supply and Sanitation in Developing Countries, (Washington, D.C.: USAID, 1981), pp. 121-138.
    [59]Popkin, "Malnourished Populations," passim.
    [60]C. Hsiang-Kuan, "China: The Rural Health Service," in Hetzel, Basic Health Care, pp. 121-127. N. Van Tin, "Mass Prophylaxis on a National Scale," in Twenty Five Years of Health Work, Vietnamese Studies 25(1970):21-40 (Hanoi, 1970).
    [61]Gwatkin, Health Interventions, passim.
    [62]Mosley, "Child Mortality," passim.
    [63]Grant, Health Care, passim.
    [64]D. Banerji, "Social and Cultural Foundations of the Health Services Systems of India," Inquiry, Supplement to Vol. 13(1975):70-85.
    [65]Newell, "Developing Countries," passim.
    [66]Mahler, "Preface"; Mosley, "Child Mortality"; Sharma, Basic Health Care.
    [67]Stern, "Health and Development," passim.
    [68]M. G. McGarry and J. Stainforth, Compost,

124

*Fertilizer and Biogas Production from Human and Farm Wastes in the People's Republic of China* (Ottawa: International Development Research Centre, 1978), passim.

[69]J. McMichael, "The Double Septic Bin in Vietnam," in *Sanitation in Developing Countries*, ed. A. Pacey (New York: John Wiley and Sons, 1978), pp. 110-115.

[70]Mosley, "Child Mortality."

[71]Newell, "Developing Countries," passim.

# Discussion

Okun: I wish I could feel as I ought to about the remarks that Professor Hardoy made earlier that habitat
and many of the things he feels should be emphasized are
ignored, while water supply and environment are getting
all the attention. Although we're still at the beginning of what has been called the international water
supply and sanitation decade, my feeling is that we're
getting a lot of newsprint but very little action, very
little money, and the decisionmakers do not give as high
a priority to water supply and sanitation as they would
have us believe.

Let me begin by summarizing the diseases that are
at all related to water. There are the so-called waterborne diseases with which we're all familiar--typhoid,
diarrhea, and hepatitis. Of equal importance are the
diseases attributed to inadequate quantities of water
(the hygienic diseases), such as trachoma, and scabies;
the water contact diseases, such as schistosomiasis; and
diseases such as malaria, where water is the habitat for
the vector, and where water services can do much, just
as habitat planning can, to ameliorate or even prevent
exposure to these diseases.

It may come as a surprise to this audience that one
of the great debates in our field is whether there is
great value in intervening in the water supply and sanitation sector in order to improve health. Interestingly
enough, intervening in the water supply and sanitation
sector is not accepted by the powers that be in such organizations as the Agency for International Development
and other donor agencies, even in some offices of the
World Bank and in the U.N. family of nations. Despite
the conventional wisdom that there is no hard evidence
that such intervention does work, recent epidemiological

125

studies show that improved water quality made available
to people in a community resulted in a 30 percent reduction in diarrheal disease. Provision of adequate quantities of water was shown to result in a 34 percent reduction in diarrheal disease, and the combination of the
two, providing good water in adequate quantities, was
shown to result in a 40 percent reduction in diarrheal
disease.

One of the major efforts currently being made is in
the movement toward low-cost water supply and sanitation. I want to emphasize that sanitation is often
neglected--a lot of lip service is given to sanitation,
a water supply is almost always the highest priority.
Sanitation is neglected because people won't pay for
it. They have to do it, but water is something they
want and are willing to pay for. Thus sanitation has
been very costly, particularly in urban settings, but
even in rural settings, so that considerable effort has
gone into trying to reduce the cost of sanitation. A
group in the World Bank, the Technical Advisory Group,
sponsored by the U.N. Development Program, is trying to
develop appropriate technology to reduce the cost of
sanitation in the developing world, but this is intended
primarily for rural areas.

I always instruct my students to go and stand on a
Saturday evening in front of a liquor store and observe
the dress of the people who buy the half-gallons and the
people who buy the pints, and you can see the high cost
of being poor. The poor have to pay a lot more for
their liquor than the rich. But this is much more serious in the field of water supply. The example that's
often given happens to be Lima, Peru.

It never rains in Lima. It may be misty, but it
just doesn't rain. You can plan a picnic, a baseball
game, anything you like, and be sure you can have good
weather for it. What this means, though, is that anything that grows has to be irrigated, and this makes
water supply very important. There's no water except
what runs from the melting snows in the Andes and flows
down the Rimac River. Despite that, a lot of the city
is very lush. Some of the homes have beautiful flower
gardens, and in these homes, generally, are families
that have maids and gardeners. Good water service in
Lima, providing about 150 liters per capita per day,
costs them less than one dollar per month per household.
The price has gone up recently, of course, but the order
of magnitude is about the same.

Now those who get poor service, who have no piping
to their homes, have to go a very long distance to the
river (there are no wells), or they buy from vendors.
The vendors pick up water from the public system, so the
quality isn't good, and they sell it to the households.
The use of water from vendors is about twenty-five
liters per capita per day, and the price is about three

dollars per month per household. In other words, they're paying three times more for much less water, and much poorer service. This is what characterizes water supply as different from some other health services. If they were investing the money they are now paying in a proper water system, they could get water service at lower cost and of a much better quality.

Just a few months ago, I was driving in western Kenya, and I saw some men by a river, filling kerosene tins with river water. They were putting the tins on a cart, and they would go to a village and sell the water in the village. Now western Kenya is not an arid country, but the village was sufficiently far from water that the absence of public services had created a business, though the quality of that water was very poor. In Jakarta or any of the cities in Indonesia, water selling is big business. It's a private entrepreneurial water service run by the local mafia, and people do buy the water. They have to pay, or they won't get water, and they do pay. So water is something that people are prepared to pay for. It has economic value. It is not just an agent for good health; it's a utility. In neglecting the value of water service for all the necessary household functions--drinking, cooking, cleaning, washing, and so forth--economists often provide a distorted appraisal of the health situation.

One of the things that makes the water supply problem a lot more difficult in the urban setting is that the kinds of institutions required to provide primary health care are different. In rural areas, we have seen that it would be entirely feasible for a local community working with the leadership of a health care clinic, or whatever health care unit there might be, to develop a well and a system for providing water and sanitation. The construction of latrines could be encouraged with local participation, and the minimum amount of imported materials could be brought in at relatively low cost. All that can be done in a rural community. But can you see this being done in a large city? In Cairo or Jakarta, or any of the urban areas where people are already beginning to live in multifamily housing? How can the local health unit organize to fight for the pumping system, the treatment system, the intake system, the dams, all that is required to bring water to this center of population? This requires a different kind of institution, a different kind of input, and yet it is critical for health. We saw this, again, in Peru. When the Indians were living up in the Andes, they were poorly nourished, it's true, but the danger to them of infectious disease was relatively low. But when they came down and started living together in the crowded environs of Lima, where their defecation affected the neighbors and vice versa, the health consequences were very much more serious. So the urban problems are really quite different.

Miller: Dan, would you repeat the statistics on the practical benefits of copious water as opposed to pure water?

Okun: Yes. The studies that assessed the effect of water quality concluded that there was a reduction of about 30 percent in diarrheal disease. The studies of water availability, even of rather poor quality, reduced diarrheal diseases by 34 percent. A combination of the two--there were four studies that examined both--reduced diarrheal diseases by about 40 percent.

Miller: Isn't it amazing that the effect is so small?

Okun: No, it's not amazing. What's amazing is that the statistics are at all consistent. The epidemiological studies that tried to assess the significance of these are all flawed. They're dealing with so many factors at the same time. We've just had a very controversial one that we conducted in Guatemala. We had what we thought was a great case: two villages, one village where we interceded with water supply and nutrition supplements, another one where we didn't do anything. We felt certain that we'd be able to show some impact. But the statisticians didn't agree. Some claimed there was evidence; another claimed there wasn't. It was very hard, because there were so many interfering effects. Social factors changed. This was a fairly sophisticated study. We weren't measuring just health. We were measuring nutritional factors, which is a much more sensitive measurement. It's very hard to get an accurate assessment of the impact, but there's really no question that the provision of adequate water supply is a high priority among local people.

Miller: There's an important study on North Carolina, old now, but unfairly neglected, a 1971 nutritional survey, when there was a lot of concern about the extent of hunger and malnutrition among poor families. As was found in many poor states, hunger and poor diets were extensive. The correlates of that malnutrition were carefully worked out, and, as you might expect, poor diet related to poor income and to poor education, and to lack of information and knowledge about food. But by far the best correlation was the adequacy of housing as defined by whether or not the house had running water, the capacity to refrigerate and store food, and food preparation facilities.

Moser: The fieldwork I was involved with over a five-year period was focused on the issue of low-income urban communities. I'm very interested in this reiteration of water as specifically important in urban areas. I would like to pick up on one or two points that have been made.

First of all, I think it was Jorge Enrique Hardoy who said that it is very difficult from our point of view to perceive what it is actually like to be involved in a basic survival struggle at the household level. As an anthropologist, I lived eight months in an urban community without any water, with kids, and I can tell you that it dominates the lives of women. It is an extremely important issue that determines not only all the things we have already mentioned, but also a lot of their income-earning activities. A lot of women earn money doing laundry work, particularly women with children. They are involved with all sorts of activities that use water. Water is the thing that women actually relate to each other about most. If you don't have water, you can't survive. Water is seen as integral to the business of running a household, and the business of running the household is women's business. So we're talking about the capacity to develop community action which comes from the bottom up, out of water. If you're looking at raising the standard of living as an alternative or in addition to income, you have to be much more concerned with looking at women and women's position. We're not just saying that we've got to bring women in at the project level because they're the ones that carry the water. If you're going to plan more effectively, more efficiently, you have to recognize not only the critical importance of target grouping by income levels, but also the importance of gender.

Okun: I'd like to add an area for research and something that we might think about. When development agencies go in, they generally bring full-scale projects with, at the very least, a tap in the yard or, where you have multifamily housing, as in most urban areas, a tap in every household unit. That means you have a problem with the sewers, because once you have water in the houses, that means you have to have flush toilets, and you have to have a way of getting rid of the waste. Very often this isn't included. The least healthful major city in the world today, I think, is Alexandria, Egypt, because there is no capacity to get rid of sewage. But the World Bank has been developing something that's in between, something less costly than this good water service--standpipes or standposts from piped systems. In the case I'm thinking of, the use was somewhat higher, about eighty liters per capita per day, and the cost is somewhat less than my Peruvian example. If you have pipes in the street, a standpipe might be in a typical place where people walk, and the objective might be that no household would have to go more than fifty meters to pick up their water and bring it to the house. That's a far superior system, and far less costly than comprehensive care, because lower per capita usage means that the pipes can be smaller, and also there's a lot less plumbing involved. That's the low-cost approach that the World Bank is now taking.

We have a project that tries to make these systems cost as little as possible. We don't include fire protection, don't include peak periods, and try to skeletonize the system to provide the basic service at as low a cost as possible. It may be poor service, but for many parts of the world that's all they are getting now and all they are likely to get for the next few decades. Even in an urban area, if we get pipes extended further, what happens? People still settle beyond that, and they won't have the piped water.

There's a reluctance to put pipes into such squatter communities because that legitimizes them. So we end up with illegitimate vendors, unregulated, taking water from terrible places, selling at very high cost, and no one bothers to study this phenomenon, a phenomenon that is ubiquitous around the world. There is not a publication by any of the donor agencies that examines any system of vending. Vending is indigenous, and we could institutionalize it, as in Lesotho and Maseru and other parts of the world. They have institutionalized the collection of bucket latrines from the home, a service that is provided by the city and works very effectively. It is probably the lowest cost method for providing this service when compared with the front-end cost of putting in a sewer system or even VIPs (Ventilated Improved Pit latrines--a very fancy latrine, the creation of the World Bank Technical Advisory Group). So why not institutionalize the lowest cost thing that will give the service in the first place? We have had nobody doing research on these indigenous patterns. There is nothing written about possibilities for standardizing containers, assuring the best water sources, helping with routing to make sure vendors serve all who need it. Yet, for urban areas and even for peri-urban areas, water vending may be the only supply that's available for years to come. For some small communities that have no water supply, it may be the only thing that's ever going to be available. So some kind of study of this should certainly be done.

Regarding standposts, there's a wide variety of circumstances. There are cases in Ethiopia where each standpost is a sort of sinecure that is given to retired army veterans or disabled persons. They stand there and collect the coupons, see that the water drains off properly, that the faucet isn't broken off, that people pay for the water they take. I know this can be controversial, but people have to pay for water; they're prepared to pay. That they pay water vendors if they don't have a piped system is a clear sign. In fact, one of the reasons I'm pushing to encourage the World Bank to investigate the possible regulation of water vendors is that if people are paying vendors a lot for poor service, how much more ready they will be to pay less for better service.

In Malaysia, they have standposts with meters. The local health department pays the water authority according to the meter reading. Because the community health department was paying by the meter readings, they saw to it that the standposts and the meters were operating properly and were well-maintained. In Sudan, it was very common in the desert areas to put in a deep well, a diesel pump, and one standpost. Then as people could get sufficient money, they themselves would put in pipes from the well to their homes. There are many ways to approach this. But the examples I've given show that one of the key issues in water supply is to make sure that once installed, the system will continue to operate and to be maintained properly. Just as you would never think of putting up a health clinic building without planning for health care workers to be there, in the same way you can't put up a water supply without having people to be responsible for seeing that it continues to operate. You don't need many, they don't need to be highly trained, but they need to be there. In order to assure that, they must have a steady income. In water systems we have a big advantage over health services in that we can charge by the amount of water and it is self-sustaining. The best way to begin is at the community level, however, because the people on top generally don't care.

Vapnarsky: I would like to hear your comments about the relationship between water supply and density. Normally, cities organize around a small core that grows by increasing density while most of the population goes to the suburbs, farther and farther from the core, imposing on the municipality a tremendous effort to supply water because the leading population is always ahead of the water supply system. How do you solve this problem?

Okun: You're always behind. That's why, in some cities, the rich people who decide they're going to move out beyond the city water system buy water from tankers. In Amman, all the fancy housing gets water not from pipes but from big tankers. Rich people will find a way to get water. In the United States, the center city is the poor part of the city, and the suburbs are the well-to-do, mainly because we've made water easily available in the suburbs. But in Latin America, the rich people live in the center part of the city and the poor people congregate in the suburbs. In the center city, all the services are available and the property values are very high. The poor people are forced to the outside. But from a technical point of view, and even from a cost point of view, keeping up with growth is not a problem. The problem is organizing for it and having the money up front for it.

Vapnarsky: Going back to your study of the Lima situation, what would happen if you were to increase the cost of good water service disproportionately and use the increased cash flow for construction of expanded infrastructure?

Okun: Yes, we have the same suggestion here in the United States with electricity and other things. I happen to be against using water supply as a method for income redistribution. Water supply is so important that I'd rather get it to where it has to go and have people pay their fair share, not have to subsidize because they want good water service. Subsidies should come in other ways. They shouldn't be hidden, because then you have trouble getting the money to keep something going if the subsidies are buried in the service.

Vapnarsky: Okay, but if you have a higher rate paid by the high- or middle-income group, you might start filling the gaps in the system.

Okun: I think the point you're making, which is correct, is that generally, and this is particularly true in Latin America, the costs of the richer people have always been subsidized, and this is not a fair distribution of costs. If they paid the real cost, I wouldn't talk about it in terms of their subsidizing the others. The cost of getting water from standposts is substantially less, so in that case the poor are paying a little less, not much less. There's another device that addresses your point that was first introduced in Israel when water was short, but that makes sense almost anywhere and is being introduced here. You have a fixed price for a basic amount of water. For anything more than is necessary to sustain life, you charge the marginal cost, and that starts to push the price up. If the basic amount needed is, let's say, 25 liters per capita per day, and there are five people in a household, they pay a certain fixed price for the first 125 liters per day. For anything additional that might be used for irrigating gardens or for washing machines, etc., they would pay a higher price. This is done as a sound economic policy, rather than as a subsidy.

Donahue: I think that while standpipes work well, in terms of cash-flow models, some people are beginning to say that the initial cost per standpipe is horrendous. Maybe once you get beyond that, in the long run it will ultimately have the impact on health that people are looking for, so why not begin to investigate how this can be done in a feasible way? Water is clearly essential, but sanitation has to go along with it.

In terms of sanitation, when you have standpipe systems, usually, you have public latrines, and really, they don't work. There are some exceptions, some extraordinary ones, but by and large, public latrines are places you wouldn't want to go near, and poor people certainly don't want to, either. Then there is general

environmental sanitation, refuse removal, drainage. You
see this problem most clearly in the high-density urban
areas in Latin America. In one of the largest cities in
Brazil, there is no functional drainage system. Someone
did a partial planning of one, and it now is five meters
deep in garbage that will have to be cleaned out before
the problem can be solved.

If you look at the reorganization of municipal
structures for more effective management, you see that
they're following the full-service model that is good
public administration here in North America and Europe.
Yet with that cash-flow approach to service delivery,
you find that the semiautonomous or autonomous municipal
parties that provide this kind of service refuse to go
into low-income areas because people can't afford to
pay. So ultimately it's hard to see how a piecemeal
approach to these services could really come together to
have the kind of impact we hope for.

Okun: In the United States we never had any great
desire to pay for sewage disposal, either, and what is
now being done is to attach the fee for that to the
water bill. If you get the water, then you have to pay
to get rid of it, and it's all one bill. That can also
be done to provide funds for whatever kind of sewage
system--attach it to the water system service.

The matter of refuse removal is a very serious
problem. So much depends on social structure. In Egypt,
one form is all private, tribal. They charge virtually
nothing for the privilege of collecting for salvage.
It's a very poor system, actually. It doesn't work at
all well. In fact, when nobody's looking, they dump all
the refuse down the sewer system, and it's really a
mess. That is why water supply, sanitation, and refuse
disposal are not just problems of physical infrastructure. They're problems of human institutions and finances.

You asked why we shouldn't go to the full-service
package in every household. It's a matter of equity. If
there's a certain amount of money to be obtained from
some foreign financial organization, the funds will come
to the local bank for a revolving fund. You can take a
portion of that and use it for the highest service for a
few select, or you can take it and try to spread a
lower level of service to more people. Even if the
latter seems less economical in the long run, is it more
equitable?

Donahue: One other thing is the need to have
essential health education as part of water supply.
It's really the same thing. If you do water supply, you
must do health education. You can't do effective health
education without some effective community organization
in place, whether it has to be stimulated, or you take
advantage of something that already exists. It really

creates a tremendous mess for engineers, because it is much more difficult to deal with the critical changes.

There's no clearer evidence for the importance of community education vis-à-vis water and sanitation than maintenance of systems after they're put in place. With effective community organization and education, these things are much more possible; systems last longer; investment per capita is much lower over time--you don't have to recapitalize things in three years.

Okun: The agency that supplies most of the money around the world now, the World Bank, is most guilty of neglecting this aspect. I was going to Indonesia last fall, and I spoke to a man who had served in Indonesia with the World Bank, a former student. I asked him what the problems were there, so I'd be aware. He told me the problem is that we would like to get community participation, select the communities that will get the water supply based upon the community's evinced desire by whatever measures you like, educate the community as to what's required, and have the community participate in all decisionmaking, and then we would have priorities and go in there. But the agency that provides the water supply doesn't want to do that. Why? Because it slows things down. The engineers don't want to do it. Partly because (and this is one of the issues that we haven't raised yet) in a lot of these countries, the government people derive a large part of their income from money associated with these projects--corruption. If the World Bank took the extra year and a half to do the community education, to get the community participation, these government officials would lose money. The Bank wasn't willing to stick to its plan because the Bank would seem to be failing if it didn't move the money, so it's going ahead with the plan as is. Nevertheless, what you said is true--community participation is important not only to get the project started, but to make sure that it will continue to operate and be maintained.

Donahue: I think we come back to something we were talking about in terms of primary health care, in what you would call "districting," some basic building block of organizations that has relevance for several different types of sectoral functional activity. In Nicaragua, the communal development committees are a basic infrastructure that fills the need for different kinds of action, starting with literacy. It's an organizational basis for a lot of things, including health action in the country. We can talk about primary health care, we can talk about water, we can talk about sanitation and electricity--look at the work that has been done in the southern metropolitan area of Lima. These things are effective there because there's a structure. There are neighborhood organization units that are the basic primary health care unit. People from among the four or five thousand people in an eight- or ten-block area are responsible for general community planning of their own. It has nothing to do with local government structure. They are the people that make decisions about selection of people to be their community-based primary health care workers. You can go into one of the clinics and see names written down for morning and afternoon, Monday through Friday--ten people from the neighborhood, mostly women, who are there half a day a week. Again, there must be some effective means of community organization.

Okun: The only problems with that are in the larger urban settings, where water supply has to be a large engineering project. But most of our problems are extensions in an area, or village projects. The best examples of community participation, initiation, and supervision are in Malawi, in southeast Africa. They began with water coming out of springs that served quite a few villages. The only thing the government provides is plastic piping. The people do all the construction work, and they are involved from the very beginning. They need a little bit of money for one standpost in the center of each town of about thirty or forty huts. They were educated regarding this water supply and are very proud of it. They look after it. The chief of the village has the washer.

When they exhausted the possibilities of the spring water and had to go to wells, it was a little more complicated, but it's still relatively successful. An engineer missionary was really responsible for getting that started, but local participation was and is very, very important, in this as in all other things.

In some cases, there's a problem in that a lot of the engineering decisions are being made by expatriate engineers who are very fearful of being displaced by local engineers. If they implied that they needed anything, or that some local engineers might need training, they would feel that their jobs were threatened. They have very good jobs, and they don't want to risk them, regardless of what is best for the local community. You have a lot of other institutional problems, including those of getting some soft science in with the hard. It's an institutional problem, and I think that women have a big stake in upsetting the status quo.

Satterthwaite: It is also about politics. We've talked about Vietnam, China, Nicaragua, Cuba, and Ethiopia, all of which have very important primary health care systems that are models. I wouldn't choose to live in any of those countries, because I'm comparatively rich. If I didn't have primary health care services, perhaps I would choose to live in those countries. The countries on that list are the United States' sworn enemies. They're the United Kingdom's sworn enemies. You can't divorce politics from health. Cuba has the highest life expectancy in Latin America. It has the lowest death rate in Latin America. I don't want to live in Cuba--I think what they do in terms of social control is, in many ways, awful.   But they have attacked the root of poverty.  We shouldn't deny this fact.  Then you mentioned that it's very difficult to get support for water and sanitation.   Low-income housing programs have received even lower priority. What gets the buck?   Dams, roads, major infrastructure work.   Am I wrong?

Okun:  You may be interested to know that a couple of weeks ago the World Bank decided to put urban affairs and water together, so they can share the bottom of the list.

# CHAPTER 7

# Alternative Settlement Systems and National Development Policy

## CESAR A. VAPNARSKY

Why should national development policies in Third World countries be diverted away from large cities to "small towns and intermediate cities?"[1] Economists have not yet reached any agreement as to whether there is an upper population city-size boundary above which diseconomies overcome scale economies. Let us assume that the present dominating trend in a given Third World country undergoing an increasing population concentration in large cities is to concentrate investments for economic development in those large cities. Let us assume that overall development in that country can be achieved with equal economic efficiency either by letting that trend go on or by diversifying investments among a wider range of cities and towns and excluding the largest cities. In the former case, people would continue to move to those privileged large cities to gain access to labor markets and other facilities. In the latter case, only a complex, new kind of policy to create jobs and facilities in those smaller cities and towns would be put into practice. Continuing the present trend would seem a highly convenient policy. The status quo would remain intact and the financial, political, and administrative structures that support it would require no chagne as well.[2]

　　Thus stated, this argument resists most objections. It is our contention, however, that the original question that generated it was ill-conceived since the question was framed solely in terms of economic proficiency. To encourage the growth of already large cities on the basis of economic efficiency is to neglect the quality of the lives of the people who move to large cities under such a policy. They undergo a painful process of assimilation into the new metropolitan environment and find themselves cut off from their cultural and emotional origins. Their migration to large cities contributes to the stagnation of the smaller communities with their valuable ways of life. In addition, the people who do not move are bound to a community that offers neither a larger and diversified labor market nor a richer variety of social services. A net social loss results because the qualities inherent in "small towns and intermediate cities" are worth preserving and the preferences of many people to continue living there (or to mover there) are worth respecting.[3]

The question that opened this discussion was posed in terms of mutually exclusive alternatives between big cities or "small towns and intermediate cities." It does not take into account either the diversity of settlement patterns that may be found around the world or the ways social scientists have tried to conceptualize those patterns and show how they can be changed. Human settlements simply cannot be classified along a single scale of size, from tiny hamlets of some tens of people to mammoth metropolitan areas of over ten million. In this classification, the existence of systems of "small towns and intermediate cities" is ignored. These "small towns and intermediate cities" can, as systems, provide the full range of advantages that supposedly are only offered in large cities (including scale economies, diversity of employment opportunities, and all kinds of facilities), while keeping other advantages, mainly social and environmental, that supposedly are only offered in isolated smaller communities. A truly isolated settlement, whether a large city or a "small town or intermediate city," is the exception rather than the rule. Human settlements are normally organized into systems of villages, towns, and cities (and open country population).

## RESTATING THE QUESTION

The actual question at issue should therefore be posed another way: Can systems of "small towns and intermediate cities" be viewed as viable alternatives to large metropolitan areas? By means of rationally allocated investments, can national economic development be fostered at least as efficiently as in large urban areas? Can other, noneconomic characteristics of "small and intermediate cities" regarded as valuable be maintained and even enhanced?

Not all "small towns and intermediate cities" in Third World countries form part of a system that is a viable alternative to a big city. On one extreme, we find vast regions so sparsely populated that a village or town arises only every hundred kilometers, and it cannot easily be ascribed to any broader, true settlement system. On the other extreme, we find smaller regions where towns or cities of relatively modest size are so close to one another and so complementary in their regional functions that, more than a system of different settlement units, they actually approach the characteristics of a single local settlement unit (the word "local" will be clarified below). If they are not visible as such, it is only because they are not a continuously built-up area, but several separate built-up areas emerging from a continuous, perhaps intensively cultivated, agricultural background.

Both extremes can be viewed as ends of a continuum. We have found examples of both, rather than intermediate cases, in our studies of the Comahue Region. Indeed, we found that in the whole of Patagonia, there are no large cities. According to the last population census (1980), none reached 100,000 inhabitants, and only two were approaching that figure.

## IMPROVING THE TERMINOLOGY

The term "local" is used in geography, biology, astronomy, etc., and its scope is therefore relative to what is to be understood as "macrolocal" and "microlocal." It has no absolute meaning. Following common usage when referring to the distribution of population over the earth's surface, it should be applied strictly in only two instances. First, to refer to the area within which a person effectively carries out his or her everyday activities, which I will call an individual local area. Second, the local settlement unit refers to the area delineated by the partially overlapping individual local areas of a set of persons.[4] The latter expression is quite generic. Hamlets, villages, towns, cities, and metropolises are the terms used in common language to refer to local settlement units. There is an inherent vagueness regarding the differences between any two successive terms in this list.[5] Does each term define only a continuously built-up area or does it define this plus those surrounding lands where some people live who satisfy their everyday needs in the built-up area or where some people work who live in the built-up area? A local settlement unit viewed as a built-up area only, I will call an agglomeration. This plus its immediate, populated surrounding lands (if they exist), I will call a local community (therefore, an agglomeration in the middle of a desert coincides with a local community). Correspondingly, the people living in an agglomeration are an agglomerated population, and the people living in the remainder (if any) of the local community are a

dispersed population. People living outside local communities will be called scattered population. They
engage in no daily interaction except as regards the
members of a single household since they live in houses
that are too far apart to allow household daily
interchange of any kind.[6]
These concepts are more accurate for our present
purposes and more basic than the customary urban-rural
dichotomy. They will be used freely in the ensuing
discussion.

## TWO EXTREME KINDS OF SETTLEMENT SYSTEMS

Along the railway line that runs from the Atlantic coast
to the Andean mountains, in the south of Comahue Region
there is a collection of small local settlement units
whose inhabitants number from 100 to around 5,000. These
settlements are almost bereft of dispersed population
since there are rarely any arable lands around the
corresponding agglomerations. The whole, huge area south
of the main region axis, the Negro River, is known as
Southern Line subregion. These agglomerations are
service centers for a widely scattered population that
raises sheep at the very low density that the aridity of
the Patagonian plateaus allows. Since this scattered
population does not belong to any local community, agglomerations in this subregion are therefore local communities. Several of them are also exploitation centers
for a few minerals not valuable nor abundant enough to
serve as the economic base for any large concentration
of people. The dispersion or paucity of natural resources in the subregion prevents any important rise in
the population of the subregion as a whole or of any of
its various agglomerations. In addition, these are so
far from one another that they do not compose any actual
system of settlements. Neither can such a system develop
by the application of modern transportation technology--
a rapid public transportation system there would be
economically unfeasible. All of these agglomerations
are supplied directly from and send their products directly outside the subregion. They do not depend upon
each other. These agglomerations and the remaining
scattered population form a human aggregate where not
much can be done to utilize its economic potential in
such a way as to make a more important contribution to
national development. On the contrary, excessive sheep
raising at the beginning of this century caused irreversible degradation of the soil quality there. It is
true that a few small subareas can sustain some agriculture, in those rare spots where a narrow stream
valley runs across the railway line, and that local
processing of wool or some mineral may create additional employment in a particular town. Unless still

unknown rich deposits of valuable minerals are discovered, it would be utopic to think of any major change
in the economic characteristics of the subregion. But
the 30 or 40 thousand people who live there are surely
required to take care of the 3 or 4 million sheep that
are raised there, to exploit the scattered mineral deposits so far discovered there, and to supply at least
certain elementary services in the area.

At the other end of the spectrum lies the Upper
Valley of Río Negro and Neuquen (core subregion of Comahue). It is a clear example of a settlement system composed of several agglomerations plus surrounding areas
of dispersed population, and in many respects the system
behaves as if it were a single local settlement unit.
It is true that recent economic trends and population
growth and redistribution indicate that such a pattern
is likely to collapse and will be replaced by a
metropolis-and-suburbs pattern. It is also true that
the Upper Valley's characteristic complementarity of
functions--which account for the subregion's behavior as
a single local settlement unit--was achieved as a result
of its peculiar settlement history. This, however, only
shows that in order to achieve similar complementarities
in other, less stringent systems of closely located settlement units, planning policies should replace spontaneous development. There are in Argentina several regional systems of settlements that are conceptually
nearer than the Upper Valley to typical "central-place"
systems. These are nevertheless capable as systems of
fulfilling the roles normally accomplished only by large
metropolises. They are, however, closer in character to
the Upper Valley than to the Southern Line settlement
pattern.

## THE UPPER VALLEY OF RIO NEGRO AND NEUQUEN

The Upper Valley settlement system spreads over an area
of approximately 700 square kilometers and had a population of more than 300,000 inhabitants in 1980. Only
some 45,000 inhabitants lived in the cultivated area,
however. Since any part of the population is in the
immediate vicinity of some agglomeration, it constitutes
a dispersed population, i.e., a population that belongs
to truly local communities. The rest, the agglomerated
population, is distributed over nearly thirty agglomerations in the size range of 100-90,000 inhabitants,
most of them nuclei of larger local communities. Seven
of these agglomerations, those having more than 10,000
inhabitants, plus an eighth (Plottier) rapidly approaching that figure, held almost 80 percent of the Upper
Valley's population. These eight will be called cities,
whereas the smaller agglomerations will be called towns.

No theoretical meaning is attached to these terms as
used here.

The whole settlement system rests upon an intensive
agricultural base made possible by a well-developed irrigation system. Fruit (mainly apples and pears) is the
major crop. Since 1957, industrial development linked
to fruit-growing acquired such momentum that the economy
is today widely recognized as mixed agro-industrial in
character. This completely new stage follows two earlier
historical cycles (alfalfa-/and fruit-growing). From the
outset, the Upper Valley's economy took advantage of the
rapidly developing Argentine agriculture for export,
specializing in increasingly intensive crops that take
the maximum possible advantage of the natural resources
--soil, water, and climate--and of the changing international demand. In this way, a modern economy of Argentine private capital, systematically reinvested in
the area, evolved. This growth was made possible, however, by the initial role played by the national state
in constructing irrigation works between 1911 and 1932.
British capital constructed a railway connection to
Buenos Aires as far back as 1897-1899. The vast periphery of the Upper Valley is a wind-swept plateau, more
arid than the Southern Line subregion of Comahue. But it
contains important oil and gas deposits whose exploitation has permitted its population to grow above 50,000
inhabitants, most of them concentrated in only two
agglomerations: Cutral Co-Plaza Huincul and Catriel. In
addition, since 1970, the construction of hydroelectric
works (the El Chocón-Cerros Colorados complex on the Limay and Neuquen rivers) has attracted populations form-
ing a few smaller agglomerations that decline as quickly
as they grow once the corresponding work is finished.
Meanwhile, this activity favors the economic and demographic growth of the subregion. Linkages between the
Upper Valley and its periphery are becoming increasingly
stronger.

## THE UPPER VALLEY AS A CENTRAL-PLACE SYSTEM

The cities and towns of a given region are generally
assumed to be arranged hierarchically into what has long
been conceptualized as a "central-place" system. It is
theoretically assumed that in a homogeneous region a
layer of dispersed population exists dedicated exclusively to agricultural activities. This population requires routine daily services at regular and close distances, giving rise to the emergence of very small population concentrations, the lowest level in the hierarchy of centers. Other services are necessary but not
required daily by the dispersed population and the
population living in those small concentrations. Only
some of the routine service locations will be chosen to

provide this second, higher level of services. Consequently, in these locations somewhat larger "central
places" will emerge. The same reasoning led to a theory
that even in a truly homogeneous plain, the population
will be distributed neither at random nor in a uniform
way but in a system of places in which population and
economic activity are hierarchically distributed.[7]

The Upper Valley may be thought of as a homogeneous
plain, since its physical basis is the bottom of a river
valley capable of sustaining similar agricultural crops
along its entire length . Its main difference from the
homogeneous region imagined by the initial theoreticians
of central-place theory[8] is that this area is easier to
conceive of abstractly as a unidimensional broad line or
ribbon rather than as a two-dimensional plain. The
places or settlements should appear at regular inter-
vals, the most important at the geometrical center of
the whole ribbon. As one goes down the hierarchy of
settlements, more and more places should appear, all of
them at regular distances from others in the same or
higher hierarchical level.

If we take an agglomeration's population as an
indicator of its level of functional importance and rank
all the agglomerations in the Upper Valley according to
population size, some sudden jumps at a few points in
the rank order suggest the presence of a five-level
hierarchical system. The first (highest) level would be
occupied by Neuquen City, and the second level by the
cities of General Roca and Cipolletti. Ten or twelve
years ago, the highest level simply did not exist. The
functions today performed by Neuquen City either had not
yet developed or were distributed among Neuquen City,
General Roca, and Cipolletti, all of which belonged in
the same hierarchical level. Almost all the functions of
macrolocal scope--i.e., subregional (serving the whole
Upper Valley) or even regional (serving the whole
Comahue region)--are still located in one or another of
these three agglomerations, but the conditions exist for
them to arise in or to move to Neuquen City, capital of
the province of Neuquen. New public offices, institutions, wholesale stores, cultural enterprises, etc. that
serve the whole Upper Valley subregion and even all (or
almost all) of Comahue are set nowadays in Neuquen.
Some that had been operating in General Roca or Cipolletti for a long time are moving to Neuquen. The
third level corresponds to the cities of Villa Regina,
Cinco Saltos, Allen, and Centenario, i.e., the present
agglomerations that have more than 10,000 inhabitants.
The town of Ingeniero Luis A. Huergo, after a long stagnation at a lower level, is at the fourth level, that
corresponds to agglomerations having 1,000-3,500 inhabitants. In this fourth level, the city of Plottier stood
for a time, though today it has surely climbed to the
third. The fifth and last level corresponds to very

small service centers having less than 1,000 inhabitants.

This hierarchy is only hypothetical. To corroborate it, detailed information would be needed (concerning number and location of retail and wholesale stores, public offices, primary and secondary schools, cultural and recreational institutions, hospitals, professionals, etc.). Nevertheless, despite its application in a few studies done on the subregion, this approach to the study of the system of settlements is not sufficient to describe the Upper Valley. This approach makes for a false view of the Upper Valley as a set of separate agglomerations (plus their surrounding areas of dispersed population) without allowing for the "incomplete" or "excessive" cluster of services offered even in the largest city of the Upper Valley.

## THE UPPER VALLEY AS A DISPERSED CITY

The services offered from a particular center for the whole Upper Valley were localized traditionally in different agglomerations, not only in Neuquen, General Roca, and Cipolletti. For many years, the only hospital in the whole subregion operated in Allen, a smaller city. This hospital was an "excessive" service, given the size of Allen, but the total lack of hospital services in the rest of the Upper Valley meant that the services offered in Cipolletti, General Roca, or Villa Regina were "incomplete." The dispersion over various agglomerations of functions serving all of them had given the Upper Valley as a whole the character of a dispersed city. A dispersed city is a system of places quite different from the classic "central-place" system,[9] a system of physically separated agglomerations that are functionally complementary. An amount and variety of services are found among the agglomerations that in a central-place system one would expect assembled in the most important city alone. Service functions are accomplished in a dispersed city that are equivalent to those normally found in individual agglomerations having a population size equivalent to the whole set of cities and towns that form the dispersed city.

## THE TRANSFORMATION OF THE UPPER VALLEY'S SETTLEMENT PATTERN

But the dispersed city character of the Upper Valley is undergoing a remarkable transformation. Its huge population growth and its increase in administrative, economic, and political functions of macrolocal scope have made the Upper Valley a truly metropolitan area, similar in functional characteristics to other regional (not

national) metropolitan areas of Argentina. Instead of
retaining its dispersed-city character, the Upper Valley
is tending toward a spatial organization of the
metropolis-plus-suburbs type. This transformation is
neither necessary from the economic viewpoint nor desirable from the environmental viewpoint.

Economically, agriculture in the Upper Valley and
exploitation of oil and gas in its periphery offer an
excellent combination for achieving a complex and
powerful agro-mining-industrial economy. The hydroelectric works that are being constructed on the Limay
and Neuquen rivers may supply abundant and cheap energy
in support of this economy. The Upper Valley is also
the core area of Comahue, a region where, despite its
vast, almost unpopulated subareas, there are other,
smaller fertile oases, lakes, and mountains that constitute a major tourist attraction, as well as lands
that are rich in oil, gas, mineral and forest reserves,
etc. These resources have so far been neglected; there
is a lack of systematic policy aimed at truly developing the whole region. Nevertheless, the already diversified economic base of the Upper Valley and the prospects of at least some new developments in the rest of
Comahue have to foster a strong population increase.
From the settlement viewpoint, the Upper Valley presents
a unique opportunity in Argentina for the development of
a metropolitan area where all functions could be
supplied that are normally found in a metropolis, an
agglomeration far more complex and normally larger than
a city.[10] This can be achieved without the area's
inhabitants having to pay in social costs for the toll a
large city takes on the quality of life--from traffic
congestion to lack of direct access to the countryside.
In order for these advantages over a large city to be
realized, it would be necessary, first, for the different metropolitan functions to be fulfilled by and
distributed among several Upper Valley agglomerations
(as is already the case). Second, the transportation
system connecting those agglomerations would have to be
efficient, neatly separated from the system connecting
the Upper Valley with the outside world, and easily
accessible to all kinds of people, especially to the
poor, who cannot afford cars.

No policies oriented towards these goals have been
implemented so far. On the contrary, the impressive
concentration of administrative, educational, and commercial functions, as well as manufacturing activities,
in Neuquen, (the largest Upper Valley city), and the
consequent population growth and physical expansion,
have taken place in a chaotic way. The platted area has
expanded beyond what would be reasonable for a much
larger population. This has created an indefinite and
unattractive townscape and made it impossible to provide
adequate network services (running water, paved streets,

garbage collection, etc.) to the whole population. In addition, the growth of Neuquen City has had direct effects on its three nearest neighbor agglomerations, since Neuquen City is nowadays the working place of many people who live in Plottier, Centenario, and Cipolletti. As a consequence, these three cities are becoming residential suburbs of Neuquen City. Among them, only Cipolletti still retains economic autonomy as the nucleus of the richest agricultural lands in the Upper Valley and as a well-developed center of manufacturing based on agricultural production. But this only means that, rather than becoming exclusively a suburb of Neuquen, it has the prospect of acquiring a mixed "suburb" and "satellite" character--i.e., keeping its industrial character while maintaining its residential appeal for people who work in Neuquen City and depend on it for any higher level central functions.

In other words, to point out that Neuquen City has doubled its population in ten years--from approximately 43,000 to 90,000 inhabitants between 1970 and 1980--is not to say enough.[11] It is true that this is the arithmetic result of comparing two successive census figures. But such a result is a consequence of a convention that, though taken for granted when studying urban growth, is convenient to set aside in this case. The convention assigns the persons enumerated in a de facto census (as Argentine censuses are) to the place where they actually stood at midnight. Had the convention been, for example, to assign them to the place where they were at 10 a.m., in 1980 a far larger fraction of the population having their homes in Plottier, Centenario, and Cipolletti (and even Cinco Saltos) would have been assigned to Neuquen City, the place where they work or study.[12] Therefore, had the last two censuses enumerated the daytime population, not the nighttime population, it would have been found that the growth of Neuquen City in the last few years has no antecedent in any other Argentine population concentration of more than 50,000 inhabitants.

Unlike many other Third World cities that have grown because there was a push from rural to urban areas, Neuquen City has grown mainly because of a continuing employment demand that draws new workers or potential workers to the city. Neuquen City is the preferred location all over Comahue for an enormous variety of economic, military, political, and cultural activities. It has been an army garrison since 1941, the political capital of a new federal province since 1957, and the administrative center for the oil exploitation that began its expansion in 1959. It is the seat of a regional university and has been since the mid-1960s, and is headquarters for the hydroelectric works begun in 1970. Neuquen City has been systematically absorbing the growth of a vast part of Comahue, the Upper Valley, and its periphery.

The city grows at a pace that outstrips its ability to supply housing facilities for the newly arrived, whether poor or not. A large proportion of the new population is constrained to seek housing in other agglomerations. This can be viewed as a favorable consequence for agglomerations having a comparatively weak economic base, such as Centenario or Plottier, which have become dormitory towns and have joined their future development to that of Neuquen City. Not so for Cipolletti, nor even for the largest of the cities in the Rio Negro portion of the Upper Valley, General Roca.[13] Here the greater distance from Neuquen City has prevented its following Cipolletti's partial transformation into a dormitory town. But both of these cities are no longer chosen as locations for new functions of subregional and regional scope. They are also being deprived of other economic, administrative, or political functions of subregional and regional scope that had long ago been established there. This has strong negative effects on their respective economic bases which, by losing the diversity that Neuquen City's base gains, become much more vulnerable to sectoral economic crises, a serious example of which is the crisis that has affected the whole Argentine fruit sector since 1979.

The transformation of the Upper Valley metropolitan area from a dispersed-city pattern to a metropolis-and-suburbs pattern is undesirable. To be convinced of this assertion requires setting aside the widely held image that only a metropolis can supply the diversity of functions--commercial, financial, administrative, educational, cultural, recreational--that the inhabitants of any local community wish to enjoy and the scale economies that no small local settlement unit can offer.

The arguments raised here against this transformation are based on the notion that it is desirable to achieve two complementary objectives: one is to ensure the future sustained economic development of a given settlement system--and consequently of the nation at large--by making the functions of macrolocal scope among its major agglomerations complementary and fostering the diversifications of other activities in all of them. The other objective is to enhance the quality of life for the whole population, present and future, of that given settlement system. This means making the labor markets and urban services accessible to all the settlement system population, particularly the poor, and protecting the system's natural and manmade environment in such a way that the settlement system may adapt to the constantly renewed needs imposed by overall economic and demographic growth.

Is it possible to avoid this transformation? The answer to this question requires that several distinc-

tions be made. In a strictly demographic sense, the
main issue is the recent population growth and the potential for future growth of the various Upper Valley
agglomerations. Since the province of the Neuquen portion of the Upper Valley has received a greater immigra-
tion, mainly young people, than the province of the
Rio Negro portion, its age structure has been more
deeply modified. This is bound to lead to a greater
natural population growth in the coming years. That is,
even in the absence of any in-migration or out-
migration, the Neuquen portion will grow more quickly
than the Rio Negro portion for several years. These
prospects raise a challenge to economic and urban
policies. A drastic change in the policies of the
national and provincial governments is needed to avoid
the negative consequences of this transformation, i.e.,
to allow the Upper Valley to fulfill its role as
regional metropolitan area of Comahue without becoming a
metropolis surrounded by residential suburbs and,
perhaps, a few dominant agro-industrial satellites.

Such drastic change in public policies should have
two objectives. One is to reinforce and diversify the
economic bases of the several cities and towns (and
their surrounding agricultural areas) so that they are
less vulnerable to negative economic impacts. The other
is to reestablish a balance among the upper level central functions (administrative, commercial, educational,
etc.) in the cities of both the provinces of the Rio
Negro and Neuquen portions of the Upper Valley, as well
as to ensure easy interaction among all local settlement
units of the Upper Valley. These two objectives should
be pursued simultaneously. Unless a well-balanced distribution of central functions among cities and a strong
interaction among them accompanies economic growth, the
settlement pattern will turn towards a metropolis-and-
suburbs type.

Considered alone, the first objective only
addresses the worst consequences of the present economic
crises and will only recapitulate the previous model of
economic growth that led, among other things, to economic concentration, excessive subdivision of the agricultural land, atomization of manufacturing among too
many and too small, inefficient plants, unnecessary expansion of built-up areas, emergence of shantytowns, and
lack of opportunities for the lower population strata to
raise their economic standing. Only if a broader
socioeconomic-environmental development is substituted
for sheer economic growth as a goal can these and other
drawbacks be avoided. This includes, first, considering
the middle- and long-term effects of present and future
policies rather than short-term effects only, and
second, thinking in social and environmental terms
rather than economic terms alone. Both conceptual
changes imply policies that deal with environmental

issues. With regard to "small towns and intermediate cities," the main environmental issue is the way natural resources are exploited.[14] But a settlement <u>system</u> is not simply a "small town or intermediate city," and consequently another crucial environmental issue is the way the settlement pattern itself develops. In order to prevent the Upper Valley from becoming an actual metropolis and allow it to retain and strengthen its character as a regional metropolitan area, protection of the environment is necessary. This protection in turn is needed to raise the population's quality of life.

Protection of the environment means first of all avoiding the invasion or deterioration of agricultural lands, so far the main regional natural resource, that often results from a chaotic expansion of built-up areas. As the total population of the Upper Valley grows, this can best be done by maintaining a balanced population among several agglomerations.[15] In this way, the expansion of built-up areas can be controlled far more easily than if one single agglomeration dominates the subregion, as in the case of the urban sprawl of Neuquen City. Most existing agglomerations of the Upper Valley could physically expand over the northern, arid plateaus that have no agricultural value. They should expand only to the extent that the additional population actually requires it, i.e., when average habitation densities are far above that of Neuquen City proper.

In other words, the quality of life of a population is enhanced not only by raising the income levels of the poor; environmental protection is also necessary. So is accessibility of services and places of employment. In this settlement system, accessibility requires a good public transportation system. It is not only a question of ensuring that all the population live in settlements where they have a job, shelter, and elementary services. It is also a question of making available to that population opportunities for changing a job, moving to another house or using any service. If labor markets and service areas are spatially restricted to small, badly interconnected Upper Valley subareas, only those who are privileged enough to commute all over the Upper Valley will have the freedom to work at a distance from their homes. In the absence of a good public transport system, people who do not have cars are limited in their choice of work, home, or social service.[16]

## THE UPPER VALLEY AS METROPOLITAN AREA
## WITHOUT A METROPOLIS

Let us put these ideas into a more convenient terminology. The potential size of an <u>individual local area</u> as defined above depends in the Upper Valley mostly on the social status of each individual. For those privileged enough to have cars of their own[17] the local area may expand at will to encompass the entire Upper Valley. For those who do not own cars, the individual local area is limited to those distances that can be covered by walking or perhaps riding a bicycle. Public transportation is expensive, almost wholly restricted to the main longitudinal axis of the subregion, and slow and uncomfortable. Consequently, among people living in towns or cities, those who are not fortunate enough to have cars and those who simply cannot drive live within highly restricted individual local areas. They cannot fully enjoy the services supplied all around the Upper Valley, nor can they have jobs or attend schools outside their town or city of residence. Naturally, the situation is worse for the equivalent sectors of the dispersed population.

The overlapping (always partial) of a more or less large set of individual local areas forms a local settlement unit. It normally consists of both agglomerated and dispersed population. The previous analysis shows that, for people with cars, the Upper Valley as a whole is equivalent to a local settlement unit. They may have daily face-to-face contacts at any point of the Upper Valley, since their individual local areas are very extended and strongly overlap. For the people who do not have cars, in the absence of a good public transport system, the Upper Valley is a clear set of separate local settlement units. They can have daily face-to-face interaction only with people whose homes are not far from theirs. The Upper Valley behaves partially as a single settlement unit, partially as a complex system of local settlement units. In everyday language, it is not wholly a city, but neither is it wholly a system of separate cities and towns.

In modern developments of central-place theory, two central-place systems are recognized: (a) a system of different local settlement units that as a whole covers a large area, and (b) a system of central places internal to a single local settlement unit. The dispersed city is regarded as a case in between.[18] But were a dispersed city like the Upper Valley to have a good public transport system, it would definitely behave as a single local settlement unit for all of its population, because the individual local areas of all the inhabitants could expand at will over the entire Upper Valley. This is an area far smaller than any large metropolis, which by definition is a single local settlement unit. (Granted that within some metropolises commuting may be long, uncomfortable, and tiresome, it is always in principle possible for all of its inhabitants.) Given the Upper Valley's far smaller population than that of a really large metropolis, and the fact that most of the Upper Valley's land is agricultural, not built-up, a good transport infrastructure--not only paved roads but also

the existing, almost totally neglected railroad--
complemented by a good system of buses and trains would
make for far easier and more rapid commutation than in
any actual metropolis. The Upper Valley would thus behave not for some but for all as a single local settlement unit; it would in fact economically and socially be
a single local settlement unit. But it would at the
same time retain its physical character of agricultural
area interrupted here and there by moderately sized
built-up areas that together cover a negligible fraction
of the total land. It would be, to state it briefly, a
metropolitan area without a metropolis. The advantages
of both the large metropolis and the small town would be
brought together.

Thus, in the Upper Valley, overcoming the so-called
"friction of space" removes one aspect of social deprivation, namely, a lack of physical access to employment
places and spatially fixed services. Granted, this is
not the root of social inequality at large. Social
problems cannot be solved simply by changing the location of things and persons or by diminishing the friction of space, but one source of social deprivation can
be altered, a source directly related to the way settlement patterns evolve.

A metropolis is not the only way to make services
and employment alternatives physically accessible to all
kinds of people. A large, closely interconnected population may be required to that end, but it does not follow that it has to inhabit a single, continuous built-up
area.

**GENERALIZING THE ARGUMENT**

It may be objected that the dispersed-city settlement
pattern still characterizing the Upper Valley is exceptional. We have discussed it here at some length mainly
because it is the empirical case we know best, realizing
however that there are not many true dispersed cities
all around the world. But the Upper Valley is an example of one extreme in a continuum of settlement systems
ordered according to their viability as possible
alternatives to the metropolis as channels for national
development. This viability means that they must be
able to fulfill all the functions that a metropolis does
and, in addition, present some advantages over metropolises, not necessarily economic but social and environmental.

Many typical central-place settlement systems that
are not dispersed cities are, however, close to this end
of our continuum. Appropriate public policies may mul-
tiply their potentials as labor markets and service systems without having to change their character as sets of
physically separate agglomerations. One of the obvious

examples in Argentina is the system including three
cities--Tandil, Olavarría, and Azul--located around the
geometric center of the Humid Pampa, the richest and
most populated region of Argentina. There is no individual agglomeration in the Humid Pampa having a population equal to or larger than the Upper Valley as a
whole, except on the Humid Pampa's northern boundary
(Córdoba) and on its eastern coast on the Paraná-Plata
rivers and the Atlantic Ocean (Buenos Aires and five
other ports). In the midst of the Humid Pampa, only one
agglomeration (Rio Cuarto) exceeds 100,000 inhabitants.
But Tandil-Olavarría-Azul have a joint population of
approximately 200,000 people. The cities form a triangle, with sides of forty to one hundred kilometers,
within which exist several smaller agglomerations that
help raise the overall population above the Upper
Valley's. These three cities have quite different functional characteristics, a feature that may help to make
them complementary and thus approach a dispersed-city
pattern. Public transportation is also a necessary pre-
requisite here for the development of such a pattern.
Some first steps have been taken in this direction,
notably the attempt to create a university with depart-
ments in all three cities, but no comprehensive plan has
been advanced so far.[19]

We take this example because this huge and
populated region, the Humid Pampa, lacks an agglomeration the size of the Upper Valley except at some of its
boundaries. Similar examples can be found in other Argentine regions and surely in other countries. The Upper
Valley of Río Negro and Neuquen is an exceptional case,
it is true; in addition, it is likely to disappear as a
case if its further growth escapes any control. But
under a rational public policy not only this clearly
dispersed city but also many systems of settlements that
did not spontaneously develop as dispersed cities may be
encouraged to behave as advantageous alternatives to the
metropolis.[20] While fulfilling a role in national
development no less important than true metropolises,
the dispersed cities may provide a far better milieu for
enhancing the quality of life and protecting the natural
and manmade environments.


## NOTES


This chapter is part of a larger collaborative study coordinated by Jorge Enrique Hardoy for the International
Institute for Environment and Development, London, that
includes people studying selected regions of India,
Nigeria, and the Sudan. The focus of the study is the

potential of small towns and intermediate cities to fulfill a role in national socioeconomic development.
[1]The phrase was adopted as a general label in the United Nations Center for Regional Development report of a meeting held at Nagoya, Japan, 26 January to 1 February 1982 (Nagoya: Meeting Report Series, no. 9, 1982).
[2]See a thorough discussion on this subject in Alan Gilbert, "The Arguments for Very Large Cities Reconsidered," Urban Studies 13, no. 1 (February 1976), pp. 27-34. An expanded Spanish version was published as "Reconsideración de los argumentos en favor de las ciudades grandes," Revista Interamericana de Planificación 9, no. 35 (Septiembre 1975), pp. 23-34.
[3]Some Latin American scholars are working within a challenging theoretical framework to identify the inherent advantages of the small community with regard to quality of life, e.g., Manfred Max-Neef, "Trabajo, tamaño urbano y calidad de vida," in Oficina Internacional del Trabajo (OIT), Centro Interamericano de Investigación y Documentación sobre Formación Profesional (CINTERFOR), Trabajo, calidad de vida y formacion profesional en las ciudades pequeñas (Montevideo: Informes, no. 97, 1980; also published in English), pp. 117-185.
[4]Elsewhere I have developed a conceptual framework within which these terms acquire full meaning. See Cesar A. Vapnarsky, "Toward Scientific Foundations for the Determination of Localities in Population Censuses," Genus 34, no. 1-2 (1978), pp. 79-129. Such elucidation is a subject matter neglected for decades by social scientists. The most valuable relevant literature was published between 1895 and 1915: e.g., Adna F. Weber, The Growth of Cities in the Nineteenth Century: A Study in Statistics (New York: The Macmillan Company, 1899; reprinted Ithaca, NY: Cornell University Press, 1963); Paul Meuriot, "De la mésure des agglomerations urbaines," Bulletin de l'Institut International de Statistique, Tome 11, 1re. livraison (1911): 157-216.
[5]Quite apart from population size considerations, a careful reading of the theoretical literature on "the city" throws some light on a purely qualitative distinction between three kinds of local settlement units: towns, cities, and metropolises. See Hans Paul Bahrdt, Die moderne Grösstadt: Soziologische Uberlegungen zum Stadtebau (Reinbeck bei Hamburg: Rowohlt Taschenbuch Verlag GmbH, 1961); Spanish version: La moderna metropolis: Reflexiones sociológicas sobre la construción de ciudades (Buenos Aires: Editorial Universitaria de Buenos Aires [EUDEBA], 1970).
[6]In "Toward Scientific Foundations" I have proposed the separation of the population of any region into "beta areas" that jointly form an exhaustive and mutually exclusive set of areas, characterized by considerations regarding closure of daily movements. Not all beta areas are local communities. Beta areas below a

certain lower population limit constitute a remainder outside any local community, i.e., scattered population. A theoretically grounded criterion is still needed to set that lower limit. In Comahue Region, it was not necessary to develop any theories toward this end because the agglomerated population by definition always forms part of local communities, and the remaining population belongs to two clearly differentiated classes: the population living in areas cultivated and under irrigation, which is fully dispersed (i.e., also belongs in local communities) and the remainder, which is fully scattered. The contrasting densities between these two classes are drastic enough to ensure the validity of this classification.

[7]A more sophisticated analysis should differentiate between "central" and "noncentral" functions of places. Old, crude approaches to the subject used to distinguish industrial cities, ports (or other break-in-transportation places), and central places. But central-place functions are naturally also accomplished in industrial cities and ports. A more detailed study of the functions fulfilled in the Upper Valley's settlements should take these distinctions into account. This study was not undertaken because even a preliminary sketch would take many pages and, especially, because I do not believe the classic central-place model gives account of this particular settlement pattern. This shall be made explicit below.

[8]I refer to the two classic theoreticians, namely, Walter Christaller, Central Places in Southern Germany (Englewood Cliffs, NJ: Prentice Hall, 1966; originally published in German in 1933); and August Losch, The Economics of Location (New Haven: Yale University Press, 1952; originally published in German in 1941).

[9]See Ian Burton, "A Restatement of the Dispersed City Hypothesis," Annals of the Association of American Geographers 5, no. 3 (September 1963):285-289.

[10]The distinction between the concepts of "metropolitan area" and "metropolis" is propounded in Cesar A. Vapnarsky, "El concepto de 'area metropolitana' como herramienta de investigación y planificación en America latina," Revista Interamericana de Planificación 8 no. 32 (Diciembre 1974):126-144. The sense there given to "metropolitan area" is akin to pioneer formulations of the concept by Norman S. B. Gras, An Introduction to Economic History (New York: Harper and Brothers, 1922), and by Roderick D. McKenzie, The Metropolitan Community (New York: McGraw-Hill Book Company, 1937). The sense of "metropolitan area" changed when it became a statistical term used in censuses simply to designate a set of administrative areas containing a legally defined city over a certain population threshold (in the United States, 50,000 inhabitants). This has contributed to a loss of the original meaning of the

term, which does not refer primarily to population size of a place but to its area of influence. A consequence of adopting such a purely statistical meaning in social research was to lose sight of a valuable conceptual distinction. Philadelphia, for example, undoubtedly a very large concentration of population and a commutation field, i.e., a "metropolis," has no metropolitan area of influence. Conversely, a metropolitan area may lack a metropolis--the Upper Valley of Río Negro and Neuquen.

[11]By June 1982, Neuquen City surpassed the 100,000 inhabitants mark, according to a personal communication by officials of the provincial bureau of the census. That is, after the 1980 census was taken, it has continued growing at a speed similar to that of the previous ten years.

[12]Two recent surveys on housing needs undertaken in cities of the Upper Valley revealed that the percentage of the local labor force working in Neuquen City is approximately 18 percent in Plottier and Centenario, approximately 12 percent in Cipolletti, and approximately 6 percent in Cinco Saltos. In other Upper Valley cities, the percentage is negligible. See EQUOT S.C. (directora del proyecto: Lydia Mabel Martinez de Jimenez), "Situación habitacional en cinco asentamientos urbanos de la provincia del Neuquen," 6 vol. (Neuquen, Argentina: Provincia del Neuquen, Ministerio de Obras y Servicios Públicos, Instituto Provincial de la Vivienda [IPVN], 1980, mimeo); Centro de Estudios Urbanos y Regionales [CEUR] (director del proyecto: Oscar Yujnovsky), "Caracterización, detección y análisis de las necesidades de vivienda de interés social en la provincia de Río Negro"(prepared for the Secretaria de Planeamiento of the province of Río Negro, and financed by the Subsecretaria de Estado de Desarrollo Urbano y Vivienda [SSEDUV] of Argentina, 1983, unpublished manu-population was distributed evenly over the whole Upper Their deprivation has been totally lacking, presumably years has been caused by tetanus and rickets. Though measures of community show that they are far from balancing the former. In addition to workers, a considerable number of students also come every weekday to Neuquen City from the surrounding cities. Even so, the data reveal that no city in the Upper Valley is already a truly dormitory suburb of Neuquen City; some are only in the process of becoming so.

[13]The 1980 census revealed that General Roca has around 44,000 inhabitants and Cipolletti 40,000. Apart from Neuquen City, no other agglomeration in the Upper Valley reached 20,000. According to the census official publications, General Roca had only around 38,000 inhabitants, but these publications arbitrarily exclude two areas around the city's freight railway stations which, though listed as separate localities, are in fact parts of the agglomeration of General Roca.

[14]See Mabel Manzanal, "Algunas formulaciones teóricas sobre el rol de los asentamientos medianos y pequeños" (Buenos Aires: Centro de Estudios Urbanos y Regionales [CEUR], 1982), unpublished manuscript.

[15]This does not mean that all thirty-odd actual agglomerations should have the same population. Most of the population is distributed over a few agglomerations, so the advantages of the dispersed-city pattern of settlement might be kept. If the whole population were distributed evenly over the entire Upper Valley, it would cause the loss of agglomeration economies, diminish access of the poor to labor markets and urban services, and cause irreversible damage to the physical environment, both natural and manmade.

[16]A transportation system stands apart from any other settlement network service (sewerage, running water, electricity, etc.). It accomplishes a vital role in physically and socially shaping the settlement pattern, something that no other network service does. See a thorough discussion on this in K. H. Schaeffer and Elliott Sinclair, Access for All: Transportation and Urban Growth (Harmondsworth, Middlesex, U.K.: Penguin Books, 1975).

[17]Around 1975, in the United States there was an automobile for every two persons; in Argentina there was only one for every nine. The number of cars in Argentina, however, is high among Third World countries. It has greatly increased since 1957, when the domestic automobile industry started. Even so, it is an expensive item. Within Argentina, although the Upper Valley is among the areas having a larger number of cars in relation to its population, not everybody has a car, and few families own more than one.

[18]See Brian J. L. Berry, "Cities as systems within systems of cities," Papers of the Regional Science Association 13 (1964), pp. 147-63.

[19]This example may help to visualize the relations that might be established between the agglomerations in the periphery of the Upper Valley--where there is almost no dispersed or scattered population--and those of the Upper Valley proper. The former are too unattractive and too far away to be chosen as residential places by persons who work in the cities and towns of the Upper Valley. Instead, an improved transport system might encourage people who have a job in the periphery to set their residence in cities or towns of the Upper Valley. Only a small fraction of the people who work in the periphery would take this step, and surely only among those enjoying higher incomes. The agglomerations of the periphery would thus be reduced to habitation clusters of people of modest incomes, provided that they succeed in maintaining a strong economic base. This is also their main environmental problem. One of them, Catriel, may not only persist but also grow, after oil is

exhausted, by the cultivation of the arable lands in its surroundings, the Colorado River valley. The other, Cutral Co-Plaza Huincul, for the time being depends solely on oil extraction; the only alternative is industrial development taking advantage of the high qualification of its population. Other environmental problems should also be overcome: its site is an arid plateau, deprived of water, exposed to strong winds and the devastating effects of torrential waters in time of rain. None of these two agglomerations may expect to integrate fully the Upper Valley metropolitan area. But the latter may be both a market for some of their potential manufacturing production and the area supplier of some higher level, not daily required services.

[20]A remarkable case of a truly dispersed city planned at the outset as such never materialized. It is a plan for Brasilia that did not win the first prize in the competition. See a description of it, by one of its authors, in Paulo Novaes, Ciudad y recursos humanos (Montevideo: Oficina Internacional del Trabajo [OIT], Centro Interamericano de Investigación y Documentación sobre Formación Profesional [CINTERFOR], 1976, Estudios y monografías, no. 23); published in English as City and Human Resources (Montevideo: International Labor Office [ILO], 1978, Studies and Monographs, no. 32).

# CHAPTER 8

# Poverty, Economic Stagnation, and Disease in Uttar Pradesh

## H. N. MISRA

The Third World countries have undergone great transformations in their socioeconomic structure in the last three decades. Political emancipation from colonial rule being almost complete, these countries have launched massive programs of economic development and social reforms. Depending on resource endowments, sociopolitical ideology, and structural constraints, these countries have met with different degrees of success. India, which has opted for a parliamentary democracy and a socialistic pattern of society, is rightly acclaimed to have achieved a great measure of success in many fields. The "Directive Principles of State Policy," so prominently incorporated in its Constitution, declare that the State shall strive to promote the welfare of the people by securing and protecting, as effectively as it may, a social order in which justice--social, economic, and political--shall inform all the institutions of national life. Serious doubts have been raised as to whether present developments are leading to the creation of an egalitarian society. The political awakening and economic growth that the country experienced in the last few decades were commendable by any standard; still, the achievements have been far short of expectations. A large part of the Indian masses still live in abject poverty, and it has been found that the gap between the rich and poor is widening. There has been progress in the economic field that has benefited the people unequally. Certain areas and certain sections of society have improved their living conditions, quite often at the cost of others. The present investigation measures the economic emancipation of a part of the mid-Ganga valley and analyzes the impact of economic progress (stagnation?) on the quality of life, health, and hygiene.

## THE STUDY AREA

The study was undertaken in three contiguous districts of Central Uttar Pradesh, India, Raebareli, Sultanpur, and Pratapgarh, covering an area of about 1,300 square kilometers with a total population of about six million. This particular area was selected as a representative sample of the economically depressed parts of northern India. It has a uniform surface distribution of natural resource endowments and is predominantly rural, the level of urbanization being at the rock bottom (5.2 percent). Politically, the area is interesting, as it is represented in the country's parliament by the prime minister.

The study region is located almost in the center of the most densely populated northern plain of India and presents a good sample of the population dynamics of the country as a whole. The Raebareli, Sultanpur, and Pratapgarh area registered a population increase of 25.0 percent in the last census decade (1971-1981). The rise was identical to that of Uttar Pradesh, of which it is a part (25.5 percent) and to that of the country as a whole (24.8 percent). The area has also been characterized by large-scale migration of a sizeable number of adult males to larger cities such as Bombay, Calcutta, and Kanpur in search of jobs. People of this area are reported to have gone as far as Burma, Fiji, Mauritius, South Africa, and the West Indies in search of jobs and greater opportunity. Consequently, the sex ratio (females per 1000 males) in the area is as high as 970 as compared to the average for Uttar Pradesh (886) and for the country as a whole (935). Viewed against such migration, the annual rate of population growth (2.2 percent during 1971-1981) is alarming. The rate of population growth is itself rising.

As a natural corollary to the high population growth, a result of natural increase, the proportion of population in the younger ages is increasing at the cost of the population in the working-age group. The dependency rate is naturally high. The rapid population growth has put increasing pressure on land, particularly in the absence of alternate sources of employment in the commerce and service sectors of the economy. The overall density of population was 449 persons per square kilometer in 1981, as compared with the much lower figures for Uttar Pradesh (377) and India (221).

## PROFILE OF ECONOMIC DEVELOPMENT

Agriculture is the backbone of the economy of this region. An overwhelmingly large proportion of the work force (85 percent) is engaged in agricultural pursuits, and as much as 96 percent of the gross domestic product (GDP) is contributed by the agricultural sector. A perusal of the occupational structure of the work force reveals that employment in agriculture and allied acti- vities has always been very high. In the last decade, however, there has been a slight decrease in the propor- tion of employment in the agricultural sector (from 88 percent in 1971 to 85 percent in 1981). The gain has gone not to the secondary sector but to the tertiary sector, which has increased from 8 percent in 1971 to 12 percent in 1981. Employment in the secondary sector has, in fact, decreased from 4 percent in 1971 to 2.5 percent in 1981. Similarly, the contribution of the secondary sector to the gross domestic product has decreased from 7 percent in 1960-1961 to 4 percent in 1976-1977. These facts indicate that the economy of the region has not undergone any significant structural change in the last few years and remains a subsistence agricultural eco- nomy.

The agricultural sector itself is in a depressed state, characterized by low productivity and the pre- dominance of low-value foodcrops. Land, the basic re- source of the people, is not quite intensively used. More than two-thirds of the area is under cultivation, but the total cropped area for all the crop seasons expressed as percent of the net cultivated area is as low as 136 percent. The flat terrain, the fertile soil, the abundant water supply, the excellent temperature and sunshine conditions, and above all, the great pressure of population on land warrant a much higher intensity of cropping, say about 300 percent, by increasing irriga- tion facilities and introducing technological innova- tions.

In a market-oriented economy, the decision to produce a particular crop is normally a function of the cost-benefit ratio. But in a subsistence economy, which characterizes the area under study, the decisionmaking process is conditioned by the consumption needs of the family. The predominance of cereals (covering 76 percent of the total cropped area) and pulses (12 percent) has always characterized this area. Even among the food grains, paddy and wheat each account for almost one- third of the cropped area. It is significant that the recent advances in agricultural technology have boosted the production of wheat more than that of any other crop. Consequently, the area under wheat has increased by about 200 percent in the last thirty years. Among the cash crops, sugar cane, potato, and oil seeds are the only ones worth mentioning. Though there is some impact

of the new agricultural technology on crop production
(as evidenced by the increase in the production of
wheat), the impact is not strong enough to change the
subsistence agriculture to commercialized agriculture.
The relatively small area devoted to the production of
pulses results in short supply of proteins in the
essentially vegetarian diet of the people. This has
serious implications for nutrition and health.

The real bane of the agricultural economy is the
depressingly low yield of crops. In the case of rice,
the dominant crop in the area, the yield is as low as
1,100 kilograms per hectare; for wheat, it is 1,400 kilograms per hectare. The average yield of sugar cane is
only 30,000 kilograms per hectare, and that of potato is
only 16,000 kilograms. Though there has been significant improvement in the crop yield in the last two
decades, due to improved agricultural technology (often
referred to as the green revolution), the crop yield in
the region is certainly very low, and that explains the
low income, the low purchasing power, and the poor
quality of life of the people.

It should also be kept in mind that the new agricultural technology is basically capital-intensive. It
benefits mainly the rich farmers who have large holdings
and have access to the other factors of agricultural
production like irrigation water, high-yield seeds,
chemical fertilizers, plant protection facilities, and
post harvest technology. The distribution of land is
quite skewed: about 80 percent of the farmers have very
small holdings of less than one hectare each, the average size of the land holdings being 0.34 hectares. The
small farmers, who constitute the large majority of
rural masses, have little access to the costly inputs
and have benefited little from the new farm technology.

The broad-brush picture of the economy presented
above should indicate the low level of economic development. The per capita GDP at current prices was as
low as forty-three dollars in 1976-1977. There has been
little improvement in the per capita GDP in the last two
decades. Much of the gain in economic development,
prompted by state policies and programs, has been
nullified by rapid population growth. Also, the development gains have not been shared equally by all
sectors of society. The neglect of equity and social
justice, both in policy formulation and program implementation, has resulted in the hoarding of the benefits
of economic development by a small section of the people, particularly the urban elite. The vast majority of
people, both in rural and urban areas, have been equally
bypassed by modern economic developments and are virtually in a state of economic stagnation.

The poverty and economic stagnation have their
telling effects on the quality of life, particularly on
health and hygiene conditions, as shown in the following

examination of these effects at the grass-root level in a village of Pratapgarh District.

## THE CASE OF NAUBASTA VILLAGE

Naubasta village, situated at a distance of about 40 kilometers from Bela Pratapgarh town, the district head-quarters, was selected for an in-depth study of poverty, stagnation, and disease in rural areas. It is a small village of 113 households clustered in five settlements: the main one, Naubasta, is inhabited by fifty-one families of four different castes; the other four settlements are smaller.

The total population of the village is made up of 392 males and 401 females. In view of the high rate of natural growth, the population of the village is comparatively young and 40 percent of the total population is below fifteen years of age. The family size of the households varies between one and twenty-five members, the average size being seven persons, as detailed in Table 8.1 below:

TABLE 8.1. Naubasta Village Households

| Family Size (Persons) | Number of Households |
|---|---|
| 1-4 | 31 |
| 5-8 | 53 |
| 9-12 | 15 |
| 12-25 | 14 |
| Total | 113 |

The level of literacy and education in the village is low. Only about 42 percent are literate; 21 percent have education up to the school certificate (tenth standard level), and only 9 percent are graduates. The level of literacy and education is naturally higher among the upper castes, the Brahmins and the Kayasthas, and very low in the scheduled caste, the Pasi. This may be both the cause as well as the consequence of poverty and stagnation of the socially and economically depressed community of the village. Even though primary education has been universalized and educational facilities for twelve years of schooling are available at a distance of just two hundred meters, the literacy and educational level of the scheduled caste is depressingly low. The Pasis prefer that their children tend pigs, fish, and help with farm operations and baby-sitting rather than go to school. The upper castes, with greater awareness of the value of education, take full advantage of the available educational facilities. It is interesting to note that all the thirty-four graduates belong to the upper caste, and all are employed in permanent jobs with

assured incomes, four in the adjoining villages as
school teachers and the rest in Pratapgarh, Allahabad,
and other towns. The educated people carry with them
the influences of modernization and health education,
and their staying away from the village deprives the
village folk of their influence and example.

## INCOME, POVERTY, AND INDEBTEDNESS

All the households of the village have an income of less
than Rs. 5,000 ($500.00) per capita per annum from all
sources. Leaving aside the five families in the income
group of Rs. 4,000-5,000, all in the upper castes, all
the families are economically poor, though some are a
shade better-off than others. A substantial number fall
below the poverty line of Rs. 500 that is the minimum
necessary to support the required calorie intake. Such
a low level of income and poverty explains the malnutrition, ill-health, low efficiency, low productivity,
and high incidence of disease, especially among the
children.

There is a high degree of correlation of income
level with social status (caste), land ownership,
education, and the nature of employment. The so-called
upper castes, i.e., the Brahmins and the Kayasthas, have
higher income than the backward castes (Maurya, Kurmi,
and Kahar) and the scheduled caste, i.e., Pasi. All five
families in the group of Rs. 4,000-5,000 belong to the
upper castes, the majority of them from among the
Brahmins, who are at the apex of the social hierarchy.
The scheduled caste, who are at the lowest rung of the
social hierarchy, also form the poorest of the poor in
the village. Of the twenty-five Pasi families, twenty
are below the poverty line and the remaining five are
marginally above the line. The other three social groups
that lie in the center of the social hierarchy are also
at the intermediate level in the income range. It
should, however, be noted that there are poor even among
the so-called upper castes, and there are relatively
better-off families in the backward communities too.

Since agriculture is the primary occupation of the
people in the village, the link between land ownership
and income distribution should be obvious. All the
poorest families possess very small holdings or no land
at all. Families that are in the higher income brackets
have relatively larger holdings. The general poverty of
the families could be explained by the small land-
holdings that form the crucial source of income for the
village people. The availability of farm land is as low
as 0.1 hectare per capita. The impact of small land-
holdings is accentuated by the depressed condition of
the agricultural economy due to poor infrastructural facilities. There are no sources of assured irrigation

save the thirteen unlined wells that provide irrigation
to about 1.5 hectares each. The draught power used for
drawing water from wells is all animal and human. Not
even one well is provided with the electric or diesel
motor pumps that have become so very common in other
parts of the country. The depth of groundwater availability at about 30 meters below the surface and the
economic limitations are real constraints for the poor
farmers. In fact, one family supported with income from
nonagricultural sources tried to install a diesel motor
pump some seven years back, failed miserably, and it has
yet to recover from the shock. The support from the
state that is so necessary to lift the rural poor out of
their deprivation has been totally lacking, presumably
because the local people lack political power. The
situation with regard to other inputs, such as improved
variety of seeds, fertilizers, and plant protection
measures, is no better.

The agricultural technology is still at a very low
level of development. The farming practices have undergone little change in the last three decades of planned
development. Though people now possess radios, bicycles, and watches (all are expressions of modernization), agricultural implements continue to be the same
age-old hoes, sickles, and wooden ploughs. Not even one
family has a tractor or any other modern farm equipment
worth the name (except of course, six chaff cutters).
The techniques of sowing, irrigation, fertilizer application, weeding, harvesting, threshing, and winnowing
remain the same as they have been for generations.

One important reason for the depressed state of
agriculture is the lack of interest in agriculture among
the educated families, many of whom have relatively
large holdings. The Kayastha family in particular, who
owns substantial land and who happens to be the more
educated group in the village, evinces little interest
in farming improvements. The majority are absentee farmers, in the sense that they let out the land to the
landless Kurmi and Maurya families, who are hardworking
farmers.

The practice of letting out land is more common
among Kayasthas, and lately among the Brahmins, too. It
is interesting to note that the Pasis, who are mostly
landless or possess very small holdings, are not the
beneficiaries of the let-out land primarily because of
their lack of initiative and efficiency in farming.

It has been observed that the families with a
support base of employment in the nonagricultural sectors of the economy have higher income levels. For example, all five families in the highest income bracket are
heavily supported by income from service employment. On
the other hand, none of the forty families in the lowest
income bracket have the support of income from outside
the village economy. Service employment (permanent or

quasi-permanent jobs in the nonagricultural sector, organized or unorganized) has great impact on the village economy and life in more than one way. Apart from assured income, service employment is associated with education, modernization, and change of attitudes. Most of the families with the support of service employment possess communication gadgets like radios and transistors, bicycles and watches. They are also the more literate and educated families in the village.

The poor families in the village are also indebted. As many as twenty families (fifteen Pasi, four Kurmi, one Brahmin) have taken loans from the local moneylenders at exorbitant interest of 36 percent per annum. The loans have been taken for a variety of reasons, including purchase of food and social obligations. The indebted Brahmin family took a loan from the Cooperative Bank for boring a well for irrigation. As the venture did not succeed and the poor farmer could not repay the loan, the principal and the interest have now accumulated far beyond his paying capacity. Of late, the government has initiated institutional arrangements for credit to poor farmers, particularly the scheduled caste, the landless, and marginal farmers. The procedure bottlenecks and the risk involved in using the loan scare away the poor from such credit institutions. In fact, much more important than the provision of cheap credit is the creation of the necessary infrastructure that could support and sustain the efforts of the poor farmers. Such infrastructure is unfortunately lacking.

## HOUSING, HEALTH, AND DISEASE

The poverty and economic stagnation are most prominently displayed in the housing conditions of the people. More than 50 percent of the families of the village do not have houses worth the name. They have only temporary sheds made of mud walls and thatched with the locally available plants, leaves, and straw. There are only seven families that have houses with brick walls and cemented roofs. All the houses lack sanitary fittings and toilet facilities. In addition to the poor quality of houses, the density of persons per room is quite high. Even in the mud-walled and thatched huts, there are twenty-two households/families that have four persons or more per room. It is distressing to note that the crowding is greater in the low-quality houses of the poor; in the more affluent households, the density per room is not so bad.

As a corollary to the high density per room, the availability of floor space per person is limited. As against the recommended standard of 10 square meters per person for healthy environmental conditions, as many as sixty-four families have floor space of less than 5

square meters per person. There are only nineteen households where floor space is 10 square meters or more per
person.

About general hygiene, the less said the better.
Though cattle sheds are usually separate from the living
quarters, the distance is not adequate to ensure a
healthy environment. In several cases, living quarters
and cattle sheds are huddled together, particularly in
the Pasi hamlets, where pigs and other livestock roam
around freely and defecate in the living quarters. As
all the houses lack toilet facilities, people have to go
to the open field. Often human excreta of infected
origin carries infection to crop plants and fruits that,
in turn, infect the human beings. The animal excreta of
the village is dumped in open pits, again causing serious environmental pollution, particularly during the
rainy season. None of the hamlets has proper sewerage
disposal arrangements; the waste water is drained in
open sluggish drains that provide congenial conditions
for breeding mosquitoes and injurious pathogens and
pests.

The problem of potable water is equally serious.
The handful of wells do not provide adequate water for
drinking purposes and whatever water is available, its
potability is always doubtful. Of late, two improved
quality hand pumps have been installed by the state
government. These hand pumps are inadequate to supply
drinking water to the village folk. Though these pumps
provide protection against surface contamination, under-
ground impurities cannot be ruled out. There is no institutional arrangement to determine and ensure the
quality of drinking water. As a result, many waterborne
diseases afflict the people and impoverish their health.

Low income, low purchasing power and consequent
undernourishment, poor housing conditions, and unsatis-
factory sanitation and environmental conditions together
have contributed to the poor quality of life of the
people. Even though the morbidity and mortality rates
have come down substantially due to improved medical
facilities in recent years, the people of this village
are still susceptible to different types of diseases.
In the recent survey to assess the infant and child mortality in the village, it was discovered that the greatest number of deaths of children in the last twenty-five
years has been caused by tetanus and rickets. Though
smallpox has been eradicated, measles is still quite
common in this village. The case is similar with malaria and diarrhea (Table 8.2).

TABLE 8.2: Child Mortality in Naubasta Village, 1958-83

| Cause of death | 0-1 | 1-2 | Age (Years) 2-5 | Total |
|---|---|---|---|---|
| Premature delivery | 10 | - | - | 10 |
| Tetanus | 46 | - | - | 46 |
| Rickets | 12 | 9 | 11 | 32 |
| Measles | 6 | 4 | 8 | 18 |
| Malaria and other fever | 5 | 7 | 4 | 16 |
| Diarrhea/Cholera | 4 | 1 | 2 | 7 |
| Causes unknown | 17 | 4 | 10 | 31 |
| Total | 100 | 25 | 35 | 160 |

Source:  Field Survey, 1983

Premature delivery is yet another important cause of infant mortality, primarily due to anemic conditions of the pregnant mothers. The fact that tetanus takes a heavy toll of infants' lives indicates the persistence of primitive methods of postdelivery care and lack of adequate maternity facilities.

The state of curative medicine is as poor as that of the preventive and social medical facilities. The nearest Primary Health Centers, at Lalganj and Sangipur, are located at a distance of seven and nine kilometers respectively. Lack of quick transportation, monetary constraints, and lack of awareness of the facilities are real hurdles. The two registered medical practitioners available locally are quacks. The provision of a bare-foot doctor introduced during the Janta Government is just a farce; the person assigned to this village has no training at all and seldom bothers to visit the village. In fact, most of the villagers are unaware of the very existence of any such service.

**CONCLUSION**

In the last generation of the post-Independence era, the government has adopted various policy measures to intervene in the vicious circle of poverty, economic stagnation, unemployment, malnourishment, disease, and low productivity. The measures, such as a ceiling on land-holdings, preferential treatment to scheduled caste

for government employment, universalization of primary
education, institutional arrangement for provision of
cheap credit to the rural poor, house sites for home-
less, and the like, have all met with only meager success, partly due to poor program formulation and partly
due to faulty implementation. These programs have hardly scratched the surface. What is needed is structural
change in income distribution and employment, and an
articulated infrastructural system that can generate and
sustain improvement in the living conditions of the
rural masses. Unless that is done, the slogan, "Health
for all by 2000 A.D." will remain empty words.

# CHAPTER 9

# Housing Policy and Settlement Patterns in Honduras

## LUIS SIERRA

Honduras is a small country and remarkable in that it has been so little studied as far as its general development, not to mention its particulars such as housing. Honduras is underpopulated and land rich, but the way the land resource base has been used has prevented the achievement of self-sufficiency.

Honduras is a banana republic. The fruit companies, mainly United Fruit, have shaped the nation's politics and institutions. The power of the fruit companies has been an integral part of the political process in Honduras and in all of Central America since the beginning of this century. After the 1950s, however, the international context changed in relation to the emphasis given to production in the region, the company's role in the region, and the role of U.S. capital in the diversification of economic activities in the region. At the same time, in Honduras, the end of a fifteen-year dictatorship led to a sort of liberal opening: there were elections, and there was a democratically elected government that welcomed institutional formation to deal with some of the social questions that arose as cities grew and rural inequities became increasingly difficult to deal with.

The institutional development process in Honduras was shaped largely by international interest in channelling capital--development assistance capital and also financial capital--into productive activities in the region. In the 1950s, the government facilitated the entry of assistance capital through the World Bank, the Inter-American Development Bank, and the efforts of the

United Nations to promote the development process. This changed in the 1960s with the Alliance for Progress and the Central American common market. These changes altered the character of the institutional formation process, leading to more diversification at the economic level and to the state taking a more direct role in the definition of "development" per se. In other words, development planning was an activity that the government could undertake in conjunction with other economic development processes.

In this context, housing in Honduras had always been, as far as the public sector was concerned, the work of the National Housing Institute (INV), which was created in 1957. The budget of the Honduran government for housing was less than 1 percent. Until 1963, the Housing Institute had produced approximately sixty-four units, all of them concentrated in Tegucigalpa, the capital city.

By the 1960s, the INV began to produce limited numbers of units in San Pedro Sula and intervened in some other areas. The bulk of international assistance that was channelled into the housing sector in Honduras in the 1960s was not channelled through the National Housing Institute, but rather went to labor union housing--first to the labor union of the United Fruit Company workers along the north coast, and second to a federation of labor unions of the north coast. Thus, international assistance that affected housing production did not necessarily deal with the poorest of the poor in urban centers or in rural areas.

By the 1970s, in the context of the 1974-1978 national development plan, the state began to radicalize housing policy. It began to talk of the need for a housing policy and some kind of framework to regulate the production of the Housing Institute and create other institutional mechanisms for effective housing provision in Honduras. The National Housing Finance Association (Financiera Nacional de Vivienda) was created, and it dealt mostly with middle-income housing and became the recipient of much external financial assistance. At the same time, the state created a housing committee that brought together that National Welfare Association (Junta de Bienestar Social) and other groups trying to apply a more concerted effort to the housing sphere. This streamlining addressed financial issues, but not the needs of the Honduran people. The latest initiative was an effort after the presidential elections in 1981 to tax workers to create a housing fund. This was strongly opposed by labor groups.

I undertook a socioeconomic survey in a squatter settlement in the second largest city in Honduras, San Pedro Sula, located in the banana··producing region on the north coast. The settlement that I studied was the product or the by-product of a national housing insti-

tute intervention in San Pedro Sula. The municipal government requested that the INV (Instituto Nacional de
Vivienda) intervene in the early 1970s to resolve the
housing problems of some people that had been relocated
in inner-city tenements in San Pedro Sula. But the standards for qualifying for the housing were so high that
about 40 percent of the families occupying the munici-
pally owned land turned over to the Housing Institute
were marginated by the program. These people crossed the
creek and occupied other municipal land. The population,
which was originally some 150 families, had increased to
about 350-400 families by 1978-1979.

The new settlement--created after the Housing
Institute's failure to deal with the problems involved
with the original settlement--gradually organized,
achieved legal status, and requested assistance from the
municipal government. It obtained water service and a
school that provided education for the squatters as well
as for the people who occupied the Housing Institute
project.

The initial project started by the community was
quite successful in generating community participation
and in rallying the support of most of the settlers.
They were quite enthusiastic, not only in contributing
their minimum monthly quota so that materials not produced by the community could be obtained (for example,
asbestos sheeting for the roofs and some wood), but also
in producing their own cinderblocks and using their own
labor. This started in early 1978. By early 1979, the
leaders of the community group had negotiated with the
municipal government to receive some support because the
units were not being produced fast enough. A dissident
group also had arisen within the community, composed of
low-income people, the poorest of the poor, who could
not meet the ever-increasing quotas that were necessary
to buy materials that the community could not produce.

In effect, the dissident group claimed that the
leaders had been bought out by the municipal government.
At the political level, the leaders of the community
were unable to sustain the monetary and labor contributions necessary to build the units. This scheme failed
because as the quotas started going up, people who could
not afford their quotas would sell out to other people
in the community who had more money. That brought about
speculation, as people outside the community who had
more economic stability came into the picture and
started taking advantage of that situation. The dissident group was composed of people who could not meet
quotas and who were totally disenfranchised--they could
not participate in the program.

Why can't the Honduran state effectively meet its
housing needs? Why is it that intervention by the state
effectively marginated the poorest of the poor in the
squatter settlements that proliferated in the largest

cities? What potential exists to transform policy direction in the Honduran state so that housing issues are addressed in a more equitable fashion? If policy was a failure, given the conditions in Honduras at that particular time in the 1970s, is it possible to seek a more enlightened policymaking in the current Honduran political situation?

In fact, there is very little that can be done at the policy level in a country like Honduras. In order to begin to understand the political processes at the national level, it's necessary to begin with local communities. The question raised here is the tolerance or the margins of tolerance that are possible under a militaristic, repressive regime in the current Central American situation. The capacity for reform in Honduras right now is minimal. Housing is not an issue when survival is an issue, given the military role that has been defined vis-à-vis the Nicaraguan revolution and the Salvadoran situation. It seems far-fetched to make policy recommendations with initiatives that basically only address things in the short term. There is a need to conduct fieldwork in the settlements, to understand the evolution of political power there, not only in squatter settlements and illegal subdivisions in Tegucigalpa, but also in the context of the broader struggles in Honduras. The poorest of the poor have little voice, since they're so preoccupied with making ends meet. But groups within the urban centers and some of the rural groups can be mobilized in support of some of these issues.

# Discussion

Hardoy: Luis mentioned the need to understand political evolution within the settlement power structure in relation to the national power structure. We have talked quite a lot here about community groups, about how communities organize, etc. But somehow we have implied that community organizations are relatively stable through time, and that is a mistake. A number of case studies in Latin America clearly show the relationship between the settlement power structures, how they are able to organize, the things they are able to do, and the different types of government that exist in that particular moment in that particular country. It is important to take this into consideration when one considers the possibility of improving the habitat/health equation in a particular community. The possibility for change is very much a function of the attitude governments take towards community organizations. Community organizations are not the same over periods of time. They are not stable. They have different opportunities to move in different directions, depending on changes in the political structure of the country itself.

Given the reduced scale of conventional public housing by the Honduran public housing institute, the Honduran situation clearly falls into the type of housing policy and program that is relatively common in many small countries. Practically all of the so-called "low-income" housing, conventional or not, is funded from abroad. AID, World Bank, and Inter-American Development Bank practically assume the brunt of financing these projects. It is interesting to note the influence of these bilateral and multilateral agencies in the development of priorities, in the selection of locations, in the encouragement of housing for the labor union of the

United Fruit Company.   Whatever bilateral or multilateral funds are provided for Honduras, Panama, Paraguay,
or any of these small economies, they simply represent a
minimum of what is needed for that particular country in
terms of housing, shelter, habitat.   But the payoff is a
phenomenal influence in setting policies, criteria, etc.
     My other point is something derived from my
experience in the 1950s--I was a rather active organizer
in shantytowns with my students in those days.   We organized cooperatives in squatter settlements that provided them with a full range of services--from legal to
design to technological to financial. We did quite well,
until we reached a point at which we ran into a dead
end:   that was when, after a certain period of mobilization, we were not able to provide the basis for the next
project. At that point, the community's organization
started to fall apart.   In other words, my experience is
that there is a very close relationship between continuous   mobilization,   group   enthusiasm,   and   concrete
achievements. The realization of community objectives
quite often depends on the attitudes and honesty of the
superlocal administration.
     Madison:   In situations where the recent history of
the nation shows a high degree of political volatility,
should strategies be more temporary?   Should what planners do be for the short term, anticipating that it's
going to change? Should we try to make a first step that
can be followed in any of several directions, depending
on what the political situation is in the next phase?
     Sierra:   There's only so much that the government
will tolerate in terms of the struggle of these people
for services or for appropriate housing. They do not represent a power bloc in the government, and since it's a
military dictatorship, or it has been a military dictatorship, it is very difficult to say, "If you'll vote
for candidate X, you will get some reforms."   That has
happened in rural agrarian reform in Honduras, but at
the urban level, it is very difficult to see that the
mobilization of these groups within the urban centers
will actually lead to policy transformation.   As far as
intervention is concerned, by either professionals or
concerned individuals, there's very little that can be
done, especially given the fact that there is so much
that is determined externally. The World Bank, IDB, and
AID determine what kinds of investment patterns exist in
urban centers, and for that matter, also the manner in
which our agrarian reform has taken place.   Our agrarian
reform has responded to some of the self-sufficiency
needs of Honduras, but at the same time it's been most
effective in expanding the agro-export base of Honduras
and tying right into the interests of United Fruit. In
terms of a temporary solution, yes, you can deal with
the immediate needs of the people, and I think we have
to do that. But at the same time, to meet an immediate

need and not realize that in the long run, no qualitative change will be brought about, is myopic.

Donahue: I think some of the earliest writing on
this is some of the best--the work of William Mangin
when he looked at the changing nature of social organization and formal community organization in squatter
settlements in Peru. When popular invasions of vacant
land took place, they were the result of successful and
skillful organization by people who planned and sometimes literally urban-planned--went into communities,
chalked out blocks, erected buildings made of simple materials (sometimes within twelve hours), opened stores,
started the process of making adobe bricks to put up
more permanent buildings. Yet those innovative people,
within a three- or four-year period, typically were out
of power. They had a piece of land, but they didn't
have any security of tenure. They had only the security
of large numbers to protect their right to stay. Those
people, in some cases, were more conservative vis-à-vis
the rest of the population, so there was a normal change
in leadership. People who lived on the physical edges
of the settlements would take a more innovative, radical
position that reflected the original positions of the
current leadership.

It's also normal to find disagreements that lead to
the formation of a new group that says, "You aren't our
legal representatives," or "You were, but you don't
stand for us now." It's a process that goes on all the
time. But there are also organizations that persist
over time, and there are different ways that groups han-
dle change in the broader context of community living.
When I arrived in Peru in the mid-1960s, there was an
extremely powerful organization, a squatter organization
in Arequipa. It was an organization of organizations.
Its president had to be taken into account in all fundamental political decisions related to water, sanitation,
planning, housing, infrastructure, investment, the
works, in that community. That doesn't mean they got
what they wanted all the time, but there was a presence
with which formal authorities had to deal. It was a mechanism that the people created themselves. You can also
see people doing this in other places, and it's
something you have to deal with, you have to take into
account. When we would go out and meet with some of the
mayors of the outlying municipalities of Arequipa, do
you know who was sitting next to the mayor? The president of this association. That's the way it was. Now I
also know that there were many conflicts internally in
the group, yet it was an operating mechanism that made
it possible to deal with people.

There's another organization of organizations in
Manila, which is very highly politicized, that actually
hired accountant consultants to come up with a proposal
technically as valid as those financed by the World

Bank. But the organization wanted a proposal based on other assumptions that the people felt were more in line with their reality. So I think that I see this as a sort of conflict resolution process, in many ways. You're trying to facilitate the process of bridging the gap between government agencies and communities and make it a more normal sort of thing, to reduce the need for constant confrontation. Examine different communities in terms of the skills they need to get on with getting the things they want. That doesn't mean that confrontation isn't called for, because it is, where appropriate. But what happens is that when there isn't much chance of radical change in the system, confrontation frequently leads to frozen positions and serious complications.

In Port-au-Prince, voluntary organizations are the major social service providers, not government agencies. They recently formed a group of about one-hundred volunteer organizations that are based on people from the local community carrying out the activities with financing from outside sources. There is a hybrid organization that is not exactly a community organization, but nonetheless is to be understood institutionally.

Part of working with these issues is realizing that you can't always plan for the long run, but you still have to have some fairly constant goals to work for. Opportunities have to be seized. In reference to Honduras, there are tremendous constraints taking place now. Our office in Guatemala City has just entered into an agreement with the Ministry of Health and some people at the municipal health levels in Tegucigalpa to bring to a significant number of large urban areas primary health care programs. Pieces of the programs were financed by AID and bilateral money, a piece of infrastructure here, a piece of infrastructure there, some water and sanitation here, and significant support from the Pan-American health representative in the country. An opportunity arose to really pull the pieces together in some consistent way and deal with an operational primary health care strategy. It was not the result of rational planning. It was not a long-term perspective. It's moving so fast that our office is juggling funds and resources to get things started ahead of time. There's a commitment to get into some of the really low-income areas, and I think people in our region are becoming concerned about the unanticipated migration into Tegucigalpa. The unanticipated urban growth figures are very high. So there are some people who are trying to work on these things, and even under those circumstances, managing to get something done.

Tulchin: It seems to me that the strategy for intervention in either health and/or habitat situations is a function of the political space available in dealing with the local community. The type of regime is a critical variable, but it's not necessarily the deter-

mining variable. Under certain repressive regimes, there
may be more space than in others. In Paraguay today,
there is actually more space for a primary health and
housing policy than there was under the same regime five
years ago, because of the dramatic socioeconomic changes
occurring in the southeastern portions of the state.
Something like one-third of the population moved in the
last five years in order to satisfy the dramatically
changed need for labor, creating cities where none existed.    There are labor unions now where none existed.
Although the type of regime is essentially the same,
there is now greater potential--I'll call it "political
space"--for moving in and dealing with local communities, even though the regime has no interest in improving the quality of life for the mass of the population.   Occasionally the national governments do adopt as
policy the designed improvement of the quality of life
in the mass of their population, and that will make our
interventions easier.   While that may be an ideal toward which you work, the strategy that has been articulated most frequently during the conference as being
the mostly likely has been intervention at the local
level.  Then the question is:  how do you perpetuate the
work?   You have to begin with the assumption that the
organization with which you work may not last very long.
Its very success may shorten its life for one of two
reasons: (a) it provides the minimal service that it set
out to provide, or (b) it runs out of political space.
In this sense, in Honduras, it becomes a threat to the
repressive regime, or represents a focal point for political activity that clearly is not acceptable to most
nonrepresentative governments.  So it's likely that many
of these organizations will have a short lifespan except
in cases when they are not politically dangerous and can
be incorporated into the political structure.

   Moser:   I think there are two outside constraints
that influence the life of community organizations.   One
is the pragmatism of many policies of resource allocation.   If there is no rational allocation of resources
on the part of national government or local government,
resources are usually allocated in terms of straight
political reward.   You are not allowing any "space" for
communities themselves to be able to plan, in the longer
term.   You make them have to take quick rewards for
quick things. I lived in a community on a mangrove swamp
that was fighting for infill--they wanted to make roads
in this mangrove swamp,.   In hygienic terms, it made no
sense to make roads unless you also installed tubes to
allow water to flow in and out. (They don't infill the
whole area, they only infill the arterial roads.)    I
told them you can't fight for infill without fighting
for tubes.   The community said, "Ha!   If we fight for
tubes, we won't even get infill.   There's no money for
tubes; tubes are not considered by the politicians a

nice flashy issue like roads. Putting in a road looks good; it gets votes, etc." So this encourages a terrifically pragmatic response to the situation.

The other constraint is the length of projects. They may only last a short time because they realize their objective. Health care is a classic example--there have been endless projects by well-known organizations, organizations that are trying very hard to get to the real needs, but have limited span, limited resources, limited allocation. This encourages a very different attitude on the part of local community organizations. In neither case is there any real change at the policy level or the program level over the whole allocation of resources. In this Ecuadoran community, during electoral campaigns, you had a whole spectrum of people coming in, all with promises, all linked to projects. These communities actually have to develop incredible political clout to see who works with whom, who's going to get in, who's going to vote.

Donahue: In Guayaquil, UNICEF has been trying to support some straightforward primary health care and preschool-age services at the institutional level. We had worked out an arrangement with World Bank for a percentage of one of their urban loans to be made available for social development actions. It required an agreement that had to be formally negotiated between two ministries. Over the past three years, there have been seven changes of ministers in those two ministries. The money is in an account to be used. No one has been there long enough to learn enough about it, or to make a decision to sign the piece of paper that permits the cash to flow.

So, do you do nothing, or do you continue to seek ways to use community organizations, to try to solve some fundamental, immediate problems? Do you assume a hard-line position and only work with countries that have the political room to do things, that fit the checklist, that are in the great gray area between one extreme or another?

Sierra: People talk about the replicability of projects, and the concern is with making something happen now. The limitations of working at the governmental level to bring about change in a country like Honduras are incredible. You can't do it. At the same time, you can't say, "Well, let's just sit back and wait for revolution." I don't agree with that either. But I think that as professionals we can play two roles--we can either reinforce that system through our actions, or we can begin to find effective ways of bringing about change. If you organize people in Honduras to try to improve housing or health conditions, that's another matter, and you really have to be politically realistic, in the sense that there are political dictates that shape your actions. As an international agency, the UN

has a different posture than, say, AID, because AID represents interests other than just the immediate interest of providing service, from what I know in Central
America.

The nature of international lending also has shaped
policies vis-à-vis the influx of those funds.    It
doesn't say, "Okay, we've got Honduras.  What does Honduras need?"  It's more like, "What does United Fruit
Company need on the North Coast so that it no longer has
to have its own workers, but can have independent pro-
ducers?  We'll promote agrarian cooperatives that produce the bananas that the company buys."  You're producing bananas for export.  But you've still got people
starving.  You've got 117 per thousand infant mortality,
you've got 60 percent illiteracy rate, you've got over
70 percent of the population living in rural areas in
abject misery.  How are you going to reorganize the
government, strictly at the internal level, given the
international fact that there are other intervening interests?

Alonso:  You have situations in which a semiformal
economy is being integrated with a general economy, and
you have others that are just at the bottom of the
barrel.  Those distinctions perhaps should be made more
sharply.  I find that the use of the word "community" is
sometimes intellectually misleading.  It's a complex
thing; as the leadership changes, the issues change, if
there's internal conflict.  I find it manipulative when
people from outside go in and "organize a community."
Perhaps it's unavoidable, and many people do it, but as
a policy I don't much like it.

Another thing that strikes me is that the notion of
community as it's being used has a certain scale--a
social scale, very often a geographic scale--and that
may not correspond to the important issues.  If your
problem is large scale, the community organization may
not be the proper vehicle.  Then, too, I think that the
variety of circumstances around the world is such that
"typical cases" may be rather rare.  You may have external events that produce radical changes, not just in
Honduras and Central America.  Look what's happened in
many parts of the world with the collapse of oil prices.
Look at Nigeria, for instance--kicking out a million
Ghanaians overnight.  What about community there?  Whose
community?  Or the situation in Assam with the Bengalis.
It's a very complicated thing.

In terms of the international agencies, it's clear
that their basic model is one of rational intervention.
They are large international organizations--people go
around in airplanes, burning $1500 in air tickets per
diem, to do something or other.  They work for months to
sign documents and dine at the local club, and so on.
They're suited to deal with large bureaucracies because
they are large bureaucracies--that's the reality of it.

Now I grant that many of the interventions are politically motivated--the input of the United States in the
World Bank is quite visible--withdrawal of support from
Allende, and things like that. But in the nature of
things, their role is well-intentioned; it has a particular difficulty because it can only deal through the
large bureaucracy. They have trouble dealing at the
retail level--not just in housing as a consumption good,
but say, housing as a production activity or food
production.

Donahue: I think there's merit in understanding one
of the reasons why so many social service attempts have
not worked: whatever was done was almost always never
near enough in terms of what was attempted for what
percentage of what population of what category. It was
conceived of miles, and hundreds of thousands of miles
in some cases, away from where the theoretical "target
group" was. There was no involvement at the community
level.

There are enough organized groups that have proven
their own capacity to be equal partners with governments, that at least get their own vested interest into
that process. People have different forms and different
levels of organization, and you respect that, as a way
of beginning these processes, and build on it. Certainly UNICEF has found that the agencies we support
work with community organizations that in almost all
cases were already in existence even before their needs
were identified by UNICEF. In some cases, there have
been supporting activities planned by the community
organizations before there was a government involved.

If an international organization has basically a
technical assistance mandate, and it has a centralized
headquarters in one country, the only way it's going to
work is to send people from where they are to where
someone wants some services. Other organizations have
huge amounts of money and a centralized decision-making
and programming bureaucracy administration. They send
out missions that go with tremendous power because of
the cash they represent, but it's a similar process.
Other organizations, because of their structure and
mandate, have cash and are decentralized, so their operating mode is quite different. But I think that you
have to look at the differences in organizations, structure, independence, where resources come from, and
understand something about the alternative ways that
organizations can operate. UNICEF has 75 percent of its
staff in Third World countries. It has national as well
as international professional staff at all of its offices. The use of resources is decided, not at head-
quarters, but at that level. These were conscious decisions by people in the organization ten, fifteen, twenty
years ago, to try and deal with some of these very
problems that you're talking about--continuity over

time, the capacity to get down into the political systems and manage limited resources better.

Miller: I think we are on tenuous ground if we think that we can engineer social organization in the way that we can engineer housing. Do we know as much as we want to about the way housing and habitation promote different kinds of social organization? Do we know what circumstances enable the development of certain kinds of social organization, which I see as different from engineering it? I'm made a little uncomfortable by the notion that social organization, important as it is, is so important that we move entirely away from concerns about the quality of housing. I am concerned about the quality of housing. I think that's a useful approach, but it seems to me there already is scholarship on the way that housing enables or promotes certain kinds of human interrelationship. Is that scholarship sufficient to form the basis for public policy concerning housing development that enables and facilitates constructive social organization of a nonengineered variety?

Hardoy: I wonder, in the most elementary type of settlement planning (site and services), what would people from let's say, Dakar, the first site and services project of the World Bank, have to say about settlement planning? What would people in La Paz, another site and services plan funded by the World Bank, have to say? Or people in Madras, where there is a phenomenal number of site and services projects going on? My point is that the potential users of those conventional houses or the potential users of these site and services funded by the World Bank may never have been asked what they have to say. Not long ago, I was in Resistencia and in Chaco (in Argentina), and I spoke with a director of a children's hospital. From his point of view, the number one priority was a site of a certain size, where people had enough land to grow fruit trees--which are not only an important part of the culture of the people who have come to Resistencia, but also important because of the food problem. Whether he is right or wrong, I cannot judge, but I was truly surprised at the approach of a director of a medical hospital to the problems of settlement planning.

Miller: I'm left a little uncomfortable with the notion that supportive, constructive, social organization is so important and so fragile, in the sense that when we cancel or interfere with a community's physical environment, we also destroy or change, often adversely, the social environment. I'm left with the feeling that there's nothing we can do about housing for fear that we will disrupt a constructive, supportive social organization. Isn't that a researchable issue? Shouldn't we be investigating how we can translocate, improve housing in ways that enable constructive social organization either to continue or to develop?

Hardoy:  I think that this is one of the research
programs that we hope to initiate.  It's truly learning
from what we often called "the planners of 50 percent of
the cities."  Finding out what they have in mind, trying
to act as almost a broker for the planning agencies,
saying "Look, this is the way the people see their city.
This is their experience. It is very valuable. This is
the culture.  These are the things we want to respect."